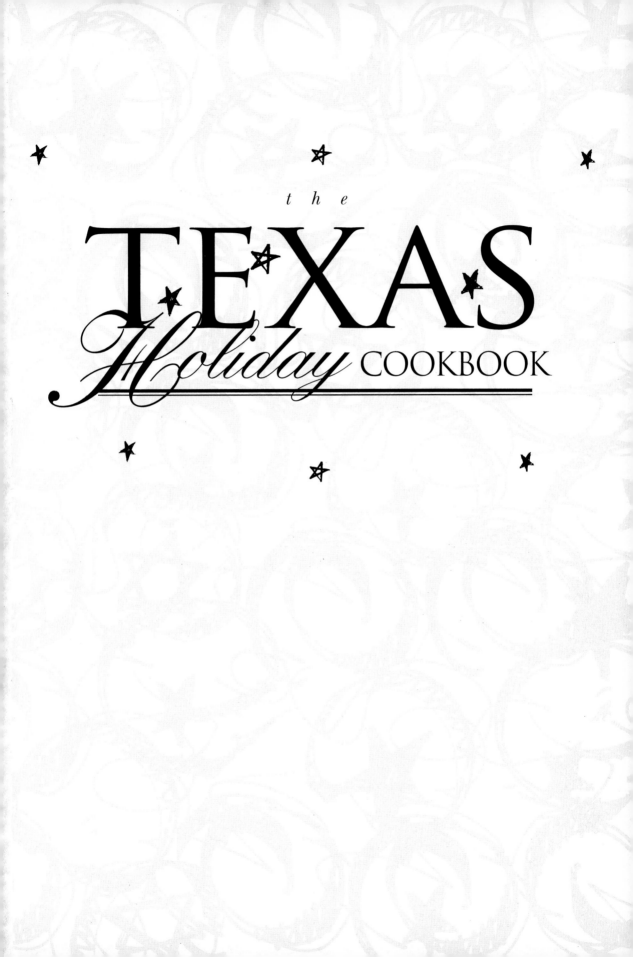

the

TEXAS
Holiday COOKBOOK

GULF PUBLISHING COMPANY
HOUSTON, TEXAS

the
TEXAS
Holiday COOKBOOK

DOTTY GRIFFITH

t h e
TEXAS
Holiday COOKBOOK

Copyright © 1998 by Gulf Publishing Company, Houston, Texas.
All rights reserved. This book, or parts thereof, may not be repro-
duced in any form without permission of the publisher.

Printed in Hong Kong

Gulf Publishing Company
Book Division
P.O. Box 2608, Houston, Texas 77252-2608

10 9 8 7 6 5 4 3 2 1

Library of Congress Cataloging-in-Publication Data
   Griffith, Dotty.
     The Texas Holiday Cookbook / Dotty Griffith; with
   foreword by Stephan Pyles.
        p.   cm.
     Includes index.
     ISBN 0-88415-869-1
     1. Holiday cookery—Texas.   2. Cookery, American—
   Southwestern style.   I. Title.
   TX739.G75   1997
   641.5′68—dc21

                                                  97-24683
                                                  CIP

Printed on Acid-Free Paper

Book design by Roxann L. Combs

DEDICATION

This book is dedicated to my Texas family who dines at
my table and taught me how to cook:
Caitlin, Kelly, Bobby, Chris, Brad, Angie, Renee, Dorothy,
Buzz, and to the memories of my father, Ed, and my
grandparents, Olga and Monroe, Netta and Edward.

ONTENTS

ACKNOWLEDGMENTS

This is a book I've longed to write since I began my career as a food journalist in 1978. Although I'd worked at *The Dallas Morning News* for six years, my time had been spent in municipal courts, on the political and education beats, in the "cop shop" (covering crime), and writing general features.

One day I found myself assigned to the food beat. More readers eat than vote, I reasoned. My audience increased exponentially. So did my knowledge of food.

Since then, I've wanted (and waited) for the opportunity to write about the cooking and flavors I grew up with: Texas cuisine. But I suspect no one would have ever dared put the word "cuisine" after "Texas" until the 1980s when American regional cuisine became recognized as distinctive, like other major cuisines with their regional variations, such as French cooking—Provencal and Burgundian, Chinese—Cantonese and Szechwan, or Italian—Sicilian and Florentine.

Southwestern cuisine, in particular, legitimized the styles of cooking common in Texas, known variously as Tex-Mex, Southern, (Gulf) Coast, country or homestyle, ranch, Hill Country, and soul. My travels over the state have introduced me to traditions and tastes far beyond my Northeast Texas upbringing in Terrell, and for that I'll be forever grateful.

I've been lucky enough to come in contact with many cooks, growers, manufacturers, chefs, producers, winemakers, grape growers, retailers, supermarket managers, ranchers, marketers, farmers, restaurateurs, hoteliers, and other wine and food professionals associated with the hospitality industries over the years. To all of them, too numerous to mention after almost 20 years, I say thank you for sharing your ideas, experience, dedication, and gusto.

I must say a special "thank you" to two cooking teachers who taught me more than I could comprehend at the time about cooking, food, and people. Kyra Effren and Nancy Parker took me under their loving wings early on when I knew more about journalism than food and accepted the sometimes difficult task of making me a fast study. I shall be forever grateful for their encouragement, confidence, and wisdom.

I'd also like to thank Chef Stephan Pyles who wrote the foreword to this book. His vision and knowledge about Texas cuisine surpasses all understanding, and I am honored to have his generous words in this book.

Many thanks go to Prissy Shaffer, whose recipe testing and food styling proved invaluable in the completion of this project. Her friendship and love are boundless. She has helped on every cookbook I've ever written and without her my work would be incomplete.

Photographer Natalie Caudill and stylist Mary Malouf, both longtime friends, captured the essence of Texas style and taste with their beautiful work. Their collaboration created stunning food photography that says more about the food of the state than my words ever could.

Although we've been close friends for years, I now count Dedie Leahy as my literary agent and art director with an eye that sees far beyond the deal.

Many thanks to Gulf Publishing's former director of the book division, William J. Lowe, editor Joyce Alff, and artistic designer Roxann Combs for their creativity, enthusiasm, and faith in this project. And to Gulf's Cheryl Smith who dreamed up the idea: a big hug.

Not the First, Not the Last

My library of Texas cookbooks is large—and growing. I've long relied on many of these books as references. They constitute an amazing bibliography of some of the best work about Texas food. Some are well-known; some aren't. Some well-respected titles aren't listed here. I mean no disrespect. Rather this list represents a very personal list of resources, not a definitive list of "best books."

The New Texas Cuisine by Stephan Pyles; *Cooking Texas Style* by Candy Wagner and Sandra Marquez; *The Melting Pot, Ethnic Cuisine in Texas* by The University of Texas Institute of Texan Cultures; *Delicioso* by the Corpus Christi Junior League; *The Only Texas Cookbook* by Linda West Eckhardt; *Celebrate San Antonio: A Cookbook,* by the San Antonio Junior Forum; *Nanny's Texas Table,* by Larry Ross; *The Try It You'll Like It Cookbook, 2nd Edition* by the New Ulm Volunteer Firemen's Auxiliary; *The Star of Texas Cookbook* by the Junior League of Houston; *From Generation to Generation* by Sisterhood of Temple Emanu-El; *The Texas Highways Cookbook* by Joanne Smith; *Christmas in Texas* by Elizabeth Silverthorne; *The Helen Corbitt Collection* edited by Elizabeth Ann Johnson.

Texas Highways magazine is also a reliable and consistent source of information about food in the state. Of particular note is a series of articles on ethnic cuisines by Howard Peacock which ran monthly during 1996.

The Texas Almanac is another valuable reference for anyone who writes about Texas history or just needs a fact about the Lone Star State.

Special Thanks

Bill and Gail Hearn Plummer opened their beautiful Texas home, built on the bank of a picturesque bend in White Rock Creek in Plano, for the location photographs in this book. Their Austin stone house, especially designed to their specifications of "casual but elegant," proved the perfect stage for these recipes to star in Texas holidays feasts. Gail, a native Texan, and Bill, who grew up as part of the Native American culture of Oklahoma, have melded their heritages in this traditional home decorated with Texas antiques and gifts from the Tonkawa Indians to Bill's family over the years. Many of the beautiful things in this book are from their personal collections. Their generosity, patience, and good humor during long days of photo shoots contributed greatly to the success of this book.

Ray Grawunder of La Mariposa in Dallas loaned much of the stunning tableware, linens, and decorative objects in the photographs. A retailer who specializes in folk art of the Americas, his trust and sharing are much appreciated.

OREWORD

When Dotty Griffith asked me to write a foreword to her book on Texas holiday cuisine, I was honored. No other journalist in the state has done more to document the diversity of Texas cuisine and liberate it from its "barbecue-only" myth. She has also become the champion chronicler of our homegrown Southwestern cuisine, which has captured the imagination of the entire country, if not the world. Dotty's 20 years in journalism puts her squarely at the forefront of the explosive interest in Texas culture.

To see the extreme diversity in the cultural and ethnic influences in Texas cookery, one need look no further than the Texas holiday table. Throughout the years, that diversity has been transformed into a homogenous union that represents the very spirit of Texas.

Like myself, Dotty is a native Texan, which means she has lived this book. It is her deeply rooted, multigenerational Texas heritage that gives this work its credibility. When she offers the reader a Thanksgiving menu of Roast Turkey, Texas Ambrosia, and Tamales, it's not a menu that has been researched and developed but one that has been lovingly recreated based on years of tradition.

Reading the chapter on Christmas makes me nostalgic for the holiday foods of my childhood. Standing Rib Roast of Beef (cattle is king) was often paired with the ultimate comfort food: Macaroni and Cheese. Where other than Texas would Roast Venison Backstrap (which suggests that Dotty had as many hunters in her family as I did) be paired with Cherry Cola salad? I've been there—eaten that!

No chapter better represents the disparate but inclusive nature that is Texas than the one on Hanukkah. It reminds me of my Jewish childhood friends who taught me to celebrate and embrace diversity. It was also a means of discovering new foods, which has been an interest all my life. Latkes with Applesauce and Sweet Noodle Kugel will always have a place in my heart.

Dotty captures the essence of Texas in her New Year's menu. Margaritas, Menudo, and Migas set the tone of this fiesta while Sugar-Baked Ham, Cheese Grits, and the obligatory Black-Eyed Peas bring a comfortable southern softness to the table. Finish the meal with Czech-inspired Kolaches, and the "big picture" of Texas cuisine begins to develop.

Since there's nothing more personal than a gift from hearth and home, the chapter on food gifts is alone worth the investment in this book. If you've never eaten or prepared the addictive southern delicacy Divinity, here's your chance.

We Texans take our holidays very seriously. If indeed we are what we eat, it's no wonder Texans have a reputation for robust personalities. Dotty's book on Texas holiday cuisine is the manual for becoming an honorary piquant Texan.

Stephan Pyles
Chef and author of *The New Texas Cuisine*
Co-owner Star Canyon in Dallas

INTRODUCTION

Texans, Their Food and Holidays

There are a great many sayings about Texas, but none captures the essence of the state any better than this one: Texas is a state of mind. And since this state has always been mine, I feel a special kinship to our people, our holidays and, of course, our food.

What makes a Texan different from those who live in and love other states? To be Texan is to be proud. Being Texan is an identity to flaunt. To enhance. To nurture. To grow into. Being Texan supercedes other ways of thinking about oneself.

Tell someone you're from, say, Illinois. You get no visceral reaction. No sense of awe or fascination. Tell someone you're from Texas. You may get a reaction to stereotypes, but you sure get a reaction. No, not everyone in Texas rides a horse on the open range or drives a Suburban to count oil wells in the front yard. But, by golly, we can play the part.

Acting Texan is part pride, part bravado, part allegiance to a way of thinking, talking, even walking, and a way of feeling about yourself, your family, your land and the image that goes with it. Texans like to say, "No brag, just fact." And we mean it.

Being Texan means embracing whatever cultural background you come from and melding it into the Texan way of doing things. Nothing illustrates this any better than serving tamales and turkey at Thanksgiving or preparing a

Hanukkah menu of latkes and chili. That's unusual, even in Texas. But the combinations are understood and embraced.

Not that Texans aren't the same from the Red River to the Gulf of Mexico, the Rio Grande to the Sabine River. Panhandle Texans, accustomed to miles and miles of open prairie, are a different breed than the urban Texans of metropolitan Houston, Dallas, San Antonio, and Austin.

East Texans, with roots in the Old South and Cajun/Creole Louisiana, and West Texans, of the big ranch culture, are from the same state but with a lot of geography and customs in between.

Yet they're all Texan.

It strikes me as a testament to the Texas persona that someone from Kansas City, Missouri, for instance, might think of himself as an Irish Catholic from the Show Me State until he moves to Texas. Transplanted, he suddenly becomes a Texan. No less Irish Catholic in family and religious-ethnic affiliation, but now a Texan.

It happens to newcomers all the time. Hence the bumper sticker: "I'm not from Texas, but I got here as fast as I could." And the proud rejoinder that simply reads: "Native Texan."

After all, Texas was once a nation unto itself. Understanding that the state once stood alone, then opted to join the Union, gives you a sense of the national pride that binds those who live within its vast borders.

When Texas was granted statehood in 1846, the annexation agreement included a clause that would allow the state to be divided into four states; perhaps what we think of as East Texas, West Texas-Panhandle, Central Texas-Gulf Coast, and the Hill Country-South Texas. But it can't ever happen. Texas then would just be another New England, a lot of small states with a regional identity.

If being Texan is a state of mind, Lone Star cuisine is a flavor and tradition all its own. It is not antebellum Southern. It is not Mexican, African-American, or German, although all those flavors find their way into Texas dishes. It isn't rancho or hard-scrabble country cuisine.

It is Texas cuisine. No less an authority than nationally respected chef Stephan Pyles, a West Texas native of Big Spring, explains: Just as there're elements of Texas style in our clothing, homes, speech and outlook, "the Texas style has influenced the way people eat and cook."

A brash fusion of condiments, touches of flavor and certain techniques distinguish Texas food from others such as the new Southwestern cuisine, which reflects a lot of New Mexican and Arizonian, as well as Texan, touches. Wonderful, but not pure Texan. That's why a Texas Christmas Eve might include sweet tamales, ham, macaroni and cheese, and rugelach.

Texas food has embraced the influences of the various ethnic groups that made the state their home. Now those influences are reflected in an amalgam called Texas cuisine.

Cornbread dressing was surely Southern in origin. Chili reflects the South Texas beef culture and the flavors of Mexico. Black-eyed peas for New Year's draws on African-American influences. And barbecue, as practiced by the masters in the beautiful Texas Hill Country settled by Germans, shows how flavorful an old country love of sausages and smoked meats can be when adapted to a frontier with beef, some pork, hardwood, spices and not much else. Of course, there are numerous other ethnic groups that have influenced Texas food—at least thirty. And more are coming all the time as Texas welcomes new Texans from Central and South America, Eastern Europe, the Middle East, and Asia.

But the two types of food that are most frequently identified with Texas are Tex-Mex and Texas-style barbecue. Both types of cooking reflect Southern/African-American, German, Mexican and cowboy ways. Jewish cuisine in Texas comes largely from the Ashkenazi traditions of Western and Eastern Europe and Russia.

Hence, the focus of this book is on the ways those ethnic traditions have come together to make up Texas cuisine, specifically the way Texans cook for the winter holidays, the most celebratory time of the year.

Starting with Thanksgiving, Texans cook up a storm until the last football game is played New Year's Day. There's no better reflection of a cuisine than the dishes that find their way to the table on seasonal holidays such as Hanukkah and Christmas.

Holiday cuisine, after all, reflects our best. The flavors on our plates are those we most love on our palates. Menus reflect traditions of the season, often common foods made special by ancestors struggling to build a new life. Menus also include foods often considered too expensive or hard-to-get except for a special occasion. Often, Texans salute their cultural heritage with a side dish, without which their holiday table wouldn't be complete. Turkey *and* tamales for Thanksgiving, for example, or perhaps maybe a platter of sausage and sauerkraut along with the turkey.

Special occasion meals reveal the touches that give a cuisine its identity: cornbread dressing, not bread stuffing for Thanksgiving, black-eyed peas with jalapenos for New Year's, Texas pecans in cakes, pies, cookies, on vegetables, in salad and roasted for nibbling. These are the culinary traditions that give a home, a family, a state the identity reflected in a holiday menu.

Holidays may be the only time all year we use our best dishes, glasses, and silverware. Yet holidays aren't stuffy or formal for most Texans. Why not sit down to a holiday feast at a table set with Lenox china, Waterford crystal, and Gorham silver wearing cowboy boots and denim?

To understand someone's holiday cuisine is to understand their culture, their values, their heritage. To join someone for a holiday meal is to become a part of their family, to taste with their palate.

Come and eat at the Texas holiday table.

Cooks' Notes:

· Oven temperatures for casseroles are set at 325° to 350° to allow flexibility for the cook. This will make it easier to double up in the oven when heating more than one dish at a time or while roasting the main course, such as turkey or roast beef, for a holiday meal.

· Many of the dishes for holiday meals—even whole meals—can be purchased as take-out or delivered by a caterer. That makes food preparation during the busy holidays much more manageable. But for those who love it, cooking during the holidays is as fun and meaningful as decorating, shopping, wrapping gifts, or any of the other tasks that some consider tedious while others eagerly anticipate. With so much available, you don't HAVE to cook. So pick your shots. Use this book to decide what you WANT to cook. Maybe it is a dish you'd like to try, one you prepare well or something you absolutely can't buy. Or maybe this book will serve you best as a menu guide. Most important. Don't feel guilty. And never—ever—apologize.

THANKSGIVING

THANKSGIVING begins the winter holiday season, a time for feasting, merriment, family, entertaining, giving and, hopefully, some receiving.

But before all the rest begins, concentrate on the feasting. "I think Thanksgiving has always been my favorite holiday," says chef Stephan Pyles, a native Texan and author of *The New Texas Cuisine,* "because the food was the main thing."

The native of Big Spring in West Texas has adapted his memories of regional favorites in his definitive cookbook and the menus at his renowned Star Canyon Restaurant. He remembers feasts with turkey, enchiladas, stuffed jalapeño peppers, and the rest of the trimmings. "My family's table was derivative of West Texas, with its Mexican, Southern, and German influences," recalls Stephan.

Indeed, Thanksgiving is the most American of holidays, and it is the one where food is the symbol of the holiday. While Texans, like most other Americans, base their Thanksgiving traditions on the Pilgrim feast of thanks that took place more than 300 years ago, Texans can also look to their own history.

The Texas Thanksgiving, a meal shared by native Texans and exploring Spaniards, is thought to have taken place about 1598. No doubt many of the dishes enjoyed at that banquet were similar to the ones enjoyed in Massachusetts in 1620 and in Texas today.

Historians believe native Texans and the Spanish explorers dined on turkey, venison, pumpkin, and corn.

Thanksgiving offers an excuse for a truly enjoyable, casual family party. In many families, everybody brings something. The day is wonderful for cooking, visiting, eating, visiting, cleaning up, visiting, and visiting some more before everyone heads home or back to their normal routine.

My family's Thanksgiving was often spent on a hunting lease in South Texas, near the town of Pearsall. One year, we added rattlesnake to our holiday table. It happened like this. My dad was 'easin' on down' one of the rough, dusty ranch roads, flanked by cactus and mesquite, in his pickup. He heard a loud thump on the driver's side front tire. He threw on the brakes and jumped out to see what he'd hit.

What he saw, was what had hit HIM—actually had hit his truck. Lucky for him.

As he opened the door and stepped out, he was startled to see a rattlesnake, easily six feet long and three inches in diameter, strike the tire again.

Dad dispatched the snake with a shotgun. He brought the big rattler home for all to see and shake their heads over the dozen rattles. Someone suggested, probably as a joke, that we have rattlesnake for Thanksgiving.

He took up the challenge. If butter and garlic can make snails taste good, why not rattlesnake? Dad flaked the white meat from the ribs and sautéed it in butter and garlic. It looked and tasted a lot like crab.

Although rattlesnake has never again graced our Thanksgiving table, that was one side dish we've never forgotten.

Dotty Griffith

THE TEXAS TURKEY

In Texas, the most difficult part of the Thanksgiving meal is timing. It is common to plan the serving time based on kick off: the Dallas Cowboys vs. the Washington Redskins. For many Texans, the rivalry has become as much a part of the holiday as turkey and dressing. Some Texans like to eat before the game; others after.

The key is making sure that the turkey and everything that goes with it are ready at the same time. For that you need to know how long it will take to thaw the turkey, have a hurry-up method in mind (just in case) and calculate the roasting time. Try to do as much in advance as possible, so that all you have to cook on the big day is the turkey. Just about everything should be a reheat or a last-step finish.

THE BEST HOW-TO IS USUALLY ON THE TURKEY WRAPPER. SOME DIRECTIONS ARE SPECIFIC TO CERTAIN BRANDS. HOWEVER, HERE ARE A COUPLE OF GENERALITIES TO GET YOU THROUGH.

DEFROST IN UNOPENED PACKAGE IN REFRIGERATOR; ALLOW 1 DAY FOR EVERY FOUR POUNDS.

SHORTCUT: PLACE BREAST-SIDE DOWN IN COLD WATER TO COVER. CHANGE WATER EVERY 30 MINUTES. ALLOW 30 MINUTES PER POUND.

IF USING A FRESH TURKEY (NEVER FROZEN), USE WITHIN 48 HOURS OF PURCHASE. STORE IN REFRIGERATOR AT 40°. PAY ATTENTION TO "USE-BY" DATE.

ROASTING the turkey is the simplest part of the meal, especially if it is a prebasted bird. I prefer the birds prebasted with broth instead of oil. The flavor of the basting liquid is less obtrusive, and the turkey is not burdened by extra calories. There are enough calories in a Thanksgiving meal, without adding any to the leanest dish on the table.

ROAST TURKEY

1	(16–18-POUND) TURKEY
2	TEASPOONS SALT, OR TO TASTE
2	TEASPOONS PEPPER, OR TO TASTE
¼–½	CUP VEGETABLE OIL
2	APPLES, OPTIONAL
1	ORANGE, OPTIONAL
1	LEMON, OPTIONAL
2	FRESH JALAPEÑOS, OPTIONAL

Preheat oven to 325°. Rinse and dry turkey. Remove neck and giblet bag from the small cavity in the front, as well as the large body cavity. Use for stock (see Gravy p. 15). Season inside turkey cavity with salt and pepper to taste. Use salt sparingly if using a prebasted turkey.

Rub exterior turkey skin generously with vegetable oil and place in a large roasting pan with shallow sides.

If desired, cut apples and orange into quarters. Cut lemons in half. Pierce jalapeños in several places with a fork. Insert apple, orange, lemon pieces, and jalapeños into cavity.

Roast turkey 15 to 20 minutes per pound. For most accurate gauge of doneness, use an instant-read meat thermometer. Temperature should read 180° when thermometer is inserted in thickest part of thigh. Juices should run clear when thigh is pierced at the thickest part, and the leg should move easily at the joint.

The turkey should be ready about an hour before dinner is served. Loosely tent with foil to keep warm, and carve just before serving.

Serves 10 to 12, with lots of leftovers.

TURKEY ROASTING GUIDE

POUNDS	HOURS
8–12	2–3¾
14–18	3¾–4½
18–20	4¼–4½
20–24	4½–5

TEXANS ARE OFTEN ON THE MOVE FOR THANKSGIVING. IF YOU DRAW TURKEY DUTY AND YOU WANT TO PREPARE IT AT HOME FOR TAKING TO GRANDMA'S HOUSE, ROAST AND CARVE IT AHEAD OF TIME. STORE IN REFRIGERATOR STORAGE BAGS. GENTLY REHEAT IN FOIL AT 300° UNTIL HEATED THROUGH (30 TO 45 MINUTES) BASTING WITH A SMALL AMOUNT OF CHICKEN OR TURKEY STOCK TO RETAIN MOISTURE.

ROAST TURKEY, P. 5

Finding a bag of giblets in a roasted turkey has scared many a Thanksgiving cook. Don't be alarmed if you forget and bake the bag in the turkey. Just take it out and make sure there's no paper left inside the turkey. Proceed as if nothing happened. In this case, confession serves no purpose. It's not good for the soul, nor for the dinner guests.

SMOKED turkeys are probably second to roasted turkeys in popularity. Of course, cooks can smoke their own on a water smoker or covered grill, and the results will be delicious. But more turkeys are probably ordered than smoked at home. And for good reason. Excellent smoked turkeys are widely available: in supermarkets, from mail order sources, local caterers, or barbecue restaurants. Yet, there's something immensely satisfying about smoking your own big bird until it is mahogany in color, juicy and flavorful.

SMOKED TURKEY

1	(10–12-POUND) TURKEY
2	CUPS PINEAPPLE JUICE
½	CUP SOY SAUCE
2	TABLESPOONS SALT
3	TABLESPOONS POULTRY SEASONING
1	TEASPOON DRY MUSTARD
1	TABLESPOON GRANULATED GARLIC
2	TABLESPOONS COARSELY GROUND BLACK PEPPER
1	TABLESPOON PAPRIKA

Rinse and dry turkey. Remove neck and giblet bag from the small cavity in the front, as well as the large body cavity. Use for stock (see Gravy p. 15). Place turkey in large reclosable plastic bag.

Combine pineapple juice and soy sauce. Pour inside cavity and over outside of turkey. Seal bag, squeezing out air. Turn bag several times to evenly coat turkey with pineapple marinade. Refrigerate several hours or overnight, turning occasionally.

Remove from refrigerator one hour before smoking. Drain marinade and discard. Combine salt, poultry seasoning, mustard, garlic, black pepper, and paprika. Sprinkle seasoning mix inside turkey, reserving some for the exterior surface. Lightly rub turkey with vegetable oil, then sprinkle with seasoning mix.

Meanwhile, prepare coals and cook turkey according to grill manufacturer's instructions. If using a water smoker, allow approximately 1 hour per pound. Replenish charcoal as needed to maintain cooking temperature.

If using a charcoal grill with lid, light coals and allow them to cook down until covered with gray ash. Push coals against sides of smoker. Place a tray of water between the piles of hot coals. Place turkey on grid over the water tray and cover with lid. Cook 30 to 45 minutes per pound, adding additional hot coals as needed to maintain medium temperature.

Temperature should read 180° when thermometer is inserted in thickest part of thigh. Juices should run clear when thigh is pierced with a fork at the thickest part.

Serves 6 to 8.

THE GRANDDADDY OF SMOKED TURKEYS IN TEXAS IS THE FAMOUS GREENBERG TURKEY FROM TYLER. SMOKED ALMOST BLACK, THESE CLASSIC EXAMPLES OF DEEP-SMOKED FLAVOR AND RICH, MOIST MEAT ARE LEGENDARY THROUGHOUT THE STATE. IF YOU WANT TO TRY ONE OF THESE CLASSICS, PHONE (903) 595-0725 OR FAX (903) 593-8129. PRICE IS ABOUT $3 PER POUND, PLUS SHIPPING AND HANDLING. SIZES RANGE FROM 6 TO 15 POUNDS.

IT is a lucky hunter who has a wild turkey to grace his or her Thanksgiving table. These noble birds are prized for their wily ways and their flavor. While domestic turkeys can be almost flavorless, their wild cousins taste as distinctive as they appear. They do not have a "wild" flavor, rather a robust, meaty flavor, with herbal undertones. But like most wild game, the meat can be dry if it is overcooked. So take care.

When I prepare wild turkey, I test the breast meat for doneness. Often the legs are too lean and muscular to be enjoyable, so safeguard the white meat. If the legs and thighs aren't quite done and you want to finish cooking them, remove from the carcass and return to the oven for 15 minutes. Let rest along with the breast, then slice. Or, save them for the stock pot.

My favorite Texas Thanksgiving sideboard holds platters of domestic and wild turkey.

ROAST WILD TURKEY

1	(8–10-POUND) WILD TURKEY OR (3–4-POUND) WILD TURKEY BREAST
2	TEASPOONS SALT, OR TO TASTE
2	TEASPOONS PEPPER, OR TO TASTE
1	APPLE
1	JALAPEÑO
1	TANGERINE
3	TABLESPOONS SOFT BUTTER
2	TABLESPOONS FLOUR
1	LARGE OVEN-ROASTING BAG

Preheat oven to 350°. Rinse and dry turkey. Season inside cavity with salt and pepper. Cut apple and tangerine into quarters. Pierce jalapeño several times with a fork.

Follow package instructions for preparing bag for roasting. Make a paste by combining butter and flour. Rub over surface of turkey. Place turkey along with apple and tangerine pieces and jalapeño in roasting bag.

Roast according to package directions, or about 2 hours for whole turkey or 1¼ hours for breast, or until meat thermometer inserted in meatiest part of breast reaches 180°. When turkey is almost done, peel back bag and roast 5 minutes longer to crisp the skin. Reserve juices to pour over meat after it is sliced to keep it moist.

Discard fruit and peppers.

Makes 6 to 8 servings.

OUR neighbors in Louisiana get the credit for Cajun-fried turkey, but Texans have embraced this cooking method as if it had come from deep in the heart. All the ingredients are there to make a Texan love it: The cooking is done outdoors, it requires special equipment, the turkey cooks fast, and it is fried.

Actually, anything as big as a turkey doesn't exactly fry when immersed in hot oil; it boils. But the end result is a moist, tender bird with a golden skin. Done correctly, it is not greasy.

FOR YEARS TEXANS HAVE LOVED TO TRY ROASTING A TURKEY IN A PAPER BAG. THIS HARKENS TO THE DAYS WHEN TURKEYS WERE TOUGH OLD BIRDS AND NEEDED STEAMING MORE THAN ROASTING. IT WAS A TIME WHEN PAPER BAGS WEREN'T AS FULL OF CHEMICALS AS THEY ARE NOW. EXPERTS RECOMMEND AGAINST COOKING A TURKEY IN A PAPER BAG, ESPECIALLY USING THOSE TECHNIQUES THAT CALL FOR ROASTING AT A LOW TEMPERATURE (BELOW 325°) FOR AN EXTENDED COOKING TIME. THE POTENTIAL FOR BACTERIAL GROWTH OR CONTAMINATION FROM THE BAG IS TOO GREAT. USE AN OVEN-COOKING BAG IF YOU WANT TO TRY THIS TECHNIQUE AND FOLLOW PACKAGE DIRECTIONS FOR COOKING TIMES AND TEMPERATURES.

Like the smoked turkey, there are plenty of places to buy a Cajun-fried turkey in most major cities. Catfish restaurants particularly like to fry whole turkeys as a holiday sideline. But if you want to try it yourself, here's how.

You'll need an outdoor cooker, usually gas powered, with a cooking pot large enough to hold 4 or 5 gallons of peanut oil and a turkey. Catalogs for outdoor equipment as well as hardware and camping stores often carry turkey-frying kits, priced about $50. They are worth the investment because they include lifters to make removing the turkey easier and safer.

There are also injector kits with syringes to shoot marinade into the turkey meat before frying. Otherwise, ample seasoning with salt and pepper, perhaps some cayenne, inside the turkey will do nicely.

This is a particularly good technique for wild turkey, because it keeps the lean meat very moist. As always with wild game, avoid overcooking. And don't let the scrawny appearance of the wild bird next to that plump domestic darling bother you. It doesn't look like a textbook turkey, but it tastes great.

TEXAS DEEP-FRIED TURKEY

1	(10–12-POUND) TURKEY
2	TEASPOONS SALT, OR TO TASTE
2	TEASPOONS PEPPER, OR TO TASTE
1	TEASPOON CAYENNE PEPPER, OR TO TASTE
4–5	GALLONS PEANUT OIL

Rinse and dry turkey. Remove neck and giblet bag from the small cavity in the front, as well as the large body cavity. Use for stock (see Gravy p. 15).

Generously season inside cavity with salt and pepper. Be as generous with the cayenne as your tastebuds allow. But don't hurt yourself; it's hot.

Heat oil in cooking pot large enough to submerse turkey in hot oil. For safety's sake, equipment for deep-frying outdoors is recommended.

Heat oil to 350°–375°. When oil is hot, using a sling of strong twine or string or a lifter that comes with a turkey-frying kit, lower turkey into hot oil. Cook about 5 minutes per pound or until meat thermometer inserted in thickest part of thigh reaches 180°.

Makes 10 to 12 servings.

For Wild Turkey: Prepare 8–10-pound wild turkey as above. Lower into hot oil and cook about 4 minutes per pound or until breast reaches 180°.

Makes 6 to 8 servings.

OUR FAMILY ALWAYS GOES TO THE RANCH (NEAR AUSTIN) FOR THANKSGIVING. WE ALWAYS GO OUT INTO THE PASTURES AND LOOK FOR THINGS TO BE THE "OFFICIAL" THANKSGIVING CENTERPIECE. EVERYBODY BRINGS BACK SOMETHING DIFFERENT, AND IT ALWAYS LOOKS BEAUTIFUL WHEN YOU PUT IT ALL TOGETHER. IT MIGHT BE A COLLECTION OF WILD FLOWERS, MAYBE A TWIG WITH A GNARLY MOSS GROWING ON IT. ONE YEAR, SOME ROCKS FULL OF HOLES LIKE HONEYCOMBS MADE UP THE BASE OF THE CENTERPIECE. WHEN THE PICKINGS ARE SLIM, WE DECORATE WITH SOME CEDAR SPRIGS AND BUNCHES OF RED BERRIES. WE'RE ALL VERY CASUAL. IT'S A JEANS-AND-BOOTS KIND OF AFFAIR.

Melinda Hill Perrin

IN Texas, it is dressing, not stuffing, and dressing is made from corn bread. End of discussion.

Some cooks may throw in some bread when they make dressing, but the traditional accompaniment to turkey is basically a corn bread mixture. The only question that may divide some families is, "Wet or dry?" Sounds like a Tennessee barbecue rib feud, doesn't it?

Most corn bread dressing tends to be on the moist side, but there are some fans who like theirs quite crisp on top, with little croutons sprouting here and there. Often this type dressing has chunks of white bread in it and always considerably less liquid.

Texas
Corn Bread Dressing

12	CUPS CRUMBLED CORN BREAD (OR EQUAL MEASURE PACKAGED CORN BREAD STUFFING MIX)
½	CUP BUTTER
2	CUPS CHOPPED ONION
2½	CUPS CHOPPED CELERY
1½	CUPS CHOPPED, UNPEELED APPLE, OPTIONAL
½	POUND BULK SAUSAGE, COOKED AND DRAINED, OPTIONAL
2	EGGS, WELL-BEATEN
5–6	CUPS (APPROXIMATELY) WARM CHICKEN OR TURKEY STOCK (MAY USE CANNED, OR SEE GRAVY P. 15)
2	TEASPOONS SALT, OR TO TASTE
1	TEASPOON PEPPER, OR TO TASTE

Preheat oven to 325° or 350°. Lightly oil a 13 x 9-inch baking dish.

Place crumbled corn bread in a large bowl. Set aside. Heat butter in large skillet over medium heat. Add onion and celery and cook until vegetables are soft, about 10 minutes.

Add sautéed onion and celery to corn bread. Add other desired ingredients, such as apple, sausage, or eggs. The addition of eggs will produce a smoother, more custard-like consistency.

Toss to combine ingredients well. Add chicken stock and mix well. For moist dressing, the dressing should be thin enough to pour into the baking dish, quite moist, but not soupy. A small amount of liquid should collect at the edges. If there is too much dressing for 1 dish, oil a smaller baking dish for the remainder.

Place in oven during last 1 to 1½ hours before serving time. Dressing is done when it achieves a firm, scoopable consistency and the top is golden brown.

Makes 10 to 12 servings.

Dry Dressing. Substitute 6 cups bread stuffing croutons for corn bread. Use about 3 to 4 cups stock or just enough liquid for crumbly consistency. Omit eggs. Proceed as above.

DRESSING is one of the Thanksgiving dishes you really should get a head start on. Bake your corn bread ahead of time. You'll need two batches for the dressing recipe. If you don't want to bake corn bread, buy corn bread squares or muffins (frozen or from the bakery).

You can crumble the corn bread and combine the sautéed vegetables with it. This may be stored in the refrigerator for several days or frozen for a month. Add stock and eggs just before baking. Or you may assemble it and bake it ahead and reheat just before serving. Place in 300° oven for 30 minutes or until heated through.

HOMEMADE CORN BREAD

1 ¼	CUPS YELLOW CORNMEAL
¾	CUP ALL-PURPOSE FLOUR, PREFERABLY UNBLEACHED
2	TEASPOONS BAKING POWDER
1 ½	TABLESPOONS SUGAR
¾	TEASPOON SALT
1	EGG, LIGHTLY BEATEN
2	TABLESPOONS VEGETABLE OIL
1	CUP MILK

Preheat oven to 425°. Grease a 9 x 9-inch pan and heat in oven while mixing batter.

Stir together cornmeal, flour, baking powder, sugar, and salt in a large bowl. In small bowl, combine beaten egg, oil, and milk. Pour into cornmeal mixture and mix just to blend ingredients. Do not overbeat.

Remove pan from oven and pour batter into hot pan. Bake 20 to 25 minutes until edges are golden and pull away from sides of pan. The center should be set.

Makes 12 (3-inch square) servings.

My mother, Dorothy Griffith, is the queen of gravy. At her house on Thanksgiving, the turkey and dressing are really just an excuse to eat her giblet gravy. She's gotten gravy-making down to an easy science.

Making the gravy unnerves many cooks. No wonder, if you save it to the very end when the turkey comes out of the oven and you're scrambling to get out the rest of the meal, hot, all at the same time.

Dorothy had a better idea: Make the gravy ahead. Add defatted pan drippings if you like, when the turkey is done, but get the gravy out of the way a couple of days ahead. It'll just get better in the refrigerator. Don't plan on making it more than a couple of days in advance, especially if you're using giblets (chopped livers and gizzards) unless you want to freeze it. But freezing adds ice crystals and forever changes the texture.

DOROTHY'S NO-FAIL GIBLET GRAVY

2	POUNDS CHICKEN OR TURKEY NECKS (OR A COMBINATION)
1	POUND CHICKEN OR TURKEY GIZZARDS AND HEARTS (OR A COMBINATION)
½	POUND CHICKEN OR TURKEY LIVERS (OR A COMBINATION)
9	CUPS WATER (DIVIDED USE)
1	CUP FLOUR
½	CUP BUTTER
½	CUP VEGETABLE OIL
3	TEASPOONS SALT, OR TO TASTE
2	TEASPOONS PEPPER, OR TO TASTE
2	HARD-COOKED EGGS, OPTIONAL

Rinse chicken necks, gizzards, and hearts. Place in a large saucepan or stockpot. Cover with 8 cups water. Bring to a boil, reduce heat to simmer. Using a large spoon, skim off foam as it accumulates during cooking.

HOW TO HARD-COOK EGGS

PLACE EGG(S) IN A SAUCEPAN AND ADD ENOUGH COLD WATER TO COVER. PLACE OVER MEDIUM HEAT AND BRING TO A BOIL. JUST WHEN WATER BOILS VIGOROUSLY, COVER SAUCEPAN WITH LID AND REMOVE FROM HEAT. ALLOW TO SET, COVERED, FOR 18 MINUTES. POUR OFF HOT WATER AND RINSE EGGS IN COLD WATER UNTIL COOL ENOUGH TO HANDLE. PEEL UNDER RUNNING WATER.

Cook until necks are soft and gizzards and hearts are tender, 2 to 3 hours.

Remove from heat and allow to cool. When cool enough to handle, strain stock into clean saucepan with lid or into a rigid plastic storage container. Refrigerate to congeal fat, several hours, up to 2 days. Freeze for longer storage.

Reserve gizzards and hearts; discard necks. Chop gizzards and hearts into ½-inch pieces. Refrigerate up to 2 days. Freeze for longer storage.

To make gravy, lift off congealed fat from stock and discard. Heat stock to liquefy; reserve.

In deep saucepan or stockpot, melt butter over medium heat. Add oil, then gradually stir in flour. Cook until flour is bubbly, reduce heat and cook until flour turns a rich brown, the color of cocoa.

Gradually add warm stock, stirring with a wire whisk to eliminate lumps. Cook until thickened to desired consistency, about 20 to 30 minutes. Season to taste with salt and pepper.

Meanwhile, rinse livers, if using, and place in small saucepan with 1 cup water over medium heat. Lower heat and simmer until livers are cooked through, 15 to 20 minutes. Remove from heat and let stand until cool. Drain livers and discard liquid. Chop livers into ¼-inch pieces.

Stir chopped gizzards, hearts, and livers into gravy. (See note.) Add chopped hard-cooked eggs, if desired. Adjust seasoning as needed.

Gravy may be refrigerated for up to 2 days before serving. Reheat to serve. Thin with defatted pan juices from turkey or with water or stock to desired consistency.

Makes 16 servings.

Note. Not everyone likes giblet gravy. For those who want plain gravy, reserve some without the giblets.

MY first recollection of cranberry sauce at Thanksgiving is the jellied variety. Slide it out of the can, slice it into rounds, then cut the rounds into wedges. It is still a staple on many Texas Thanksgiving Day tables. But fresh cranberries are more adaptable to Texas tastes. Although not native, the cranberry is something Texas cooks have taken to with enthusiasm. All sorts of native Texas ingredients—pecans, jalapeños, grapefruit and wine—can make fresh cranberry sauce a Lone Star tradition.

Mix and match these variations to suit your taste.

CRANBERRY SAUCE

2	CUPS WATER
2	CUPS SUGAR
4	CUPS (1 POUND) CRANBERRIES

Combine water and sugar in a medium saucepan. Stir until sugar is dissolved. Bring liquid to a boil over medium-high heat. Let boil about 5 minutes.

Add cranberries and cook until berries pop, about 5 minutes. Skim off any foam that accumulates. Cool and refrigerate up to 1 month.

Makes 10 to 12 servings.

Variations

- Substitute ½ cup Texas Cabernet Sauvignon, Merlot or other dry red wine for ½ cup water. Proceed as above.

- Remove seeds and membranes from a small fresh jalapeño or small serrano pepper. (Wear rubber gloves and avoid touching lips, nose or eyes after handling peppers). Finely chop pepper and add 1 tablespoon or to taste along with cranberries. Proceed as above.

- Grate 2 tablespoons peel from a Texas red grapefruit. Remove white pith and seeds from grapefruit sections and coarsely chop to measure 1 cup. Add along with cranberries. Proceed as above.

- Stir in ½ cup chopped pecans after removing from heat.

IF there is one dish almost as universal to Thanksgiving as turkey and dressing, it is Green Bean Casserole. I grew up on my grandmother's, made resplendent for the holidays with the addition of slivered almonds or sliced black olives.

GREEN BEAN CASSEROLE

1	(16-OUNCE) PACKAGE FROZEN FRENCH-CUT GREEN BEANS
1	(10¾-OUNCE) CAN CREAM OF MUSHROOM SOUP
¾	CUP MILK
½	CUP SLIVERED ALMONDS
1–2	TABLESPOONS CANNED FRIED ONION RINGS, CRUMBLED POTATO CHIPS OR TOASTED BREAD CRUMBS, OPTIONAL

Preheat oven to 325°–350°. Thaw green beans under hot running water or place in microwave just long enough to thaw. Drain well.

Stir together soup and milk in a 2-quart casserole dish until smooth. Add drained green beans and almonds, stirring gently to combine. If desired, sprinkle top with onion rings, potato chips, or bread crumbs.

Place in oven and bake until top is brown and dish bubbles at the edges, about 20 to 30 minutes.

Makes 8 servings.

Variations

· Substitute sliced black olives for almonds.

· Substitute grated Parmesan cheese for onion rings or other toppings.

· Substitute chopped toasted pecans for almonds.

SQUASH casserole, popularized in cafeterias such as Luby's and the dear departed Highland Park Cafeteria of Dallas, is a holiday tradition in many Texas homes. Ironically, it uses a summer squash.

HOMESTYLE SQUASH CASSEROLE

2	POUNDS YELLOW SUMMER SQUASH, ABOUT 4 CUPS CHOPPED
½	CUP CHOPPED ONION
4	TABLESPOONS MELTED BUTTER, (DIVIDED USE)
2	TEASPOONS SUGAR
1	TEASPOON SALT, OR TO TASTE
½	TEASPOON PEPPER, OR TO TASTE
2	EGGS, LIGHTLY BEATEN
½	CUP CRACKER CRUMBS

Preheat oven to 325°–350°. Trim ends and coarsely chop squash to make about 4 cups. Place 2 cups water in a large saucepan and bring to a boil. Add squash and cook until squash is tender, about 8 minutes. Drain well. Place drained squash in a large mixing bowl and coarsely mash with a potato masher. Drain off any liquid that accumulates.

Combine 3 tablespoons melted butter and onion in saucepan over medium heat. Cook until onion is soft, about 5 minutes. Add butter and onion to squash along with sugar, salt, and pepper. Stir in eggs.

Pour into 2-quart casserole lightly sprayed with non-stick spray. Sprinkle cracker crumbs over top and drizzle with remaining 1 tablespoon butter. Bake for 20 to 30 minutes until top is golden and edges are bubbly.

Makes 8 servings.

MASHED POTATOES *with* SOUR CREAM *and* CREAM CHEESE

6	LARGE (ABOUT 3 POUNDS) RUSSET POTATOES
1	(3-OUNCE) PACKAGE CREAM CHEESE, AT ROOM TEMPERATURE
½	CUP SOUR CREAM
¾–1 ¼	CUPS WARM MILK OR HALF-AND-HALF
4	TABLESPOONS BUTTER
1	TEASPOON SALT, OR TO TASTE
½	TEASPOON WHITE PEPPER, OR TO TASTE

Preheat oven to 325°–350°. Peel potatoes and cut into 6 or 8 chunks. Place in large saucepan with cold water. Water should just cover the potatoes when all are added. Cook over high heat until water boils, reduce heat slightly, and cook until potatoes are tender, about 15 minutes.

Drain well and return to saucepan over low heat, tossing well to cook away any remaining liquid. Using a masher or electric beater on low speed, mash potatoes, adding warm milk just until potatoes begin to take on creamy texture but before all lumps are gone.

Add cream cheese, butter and sour cream, mashing or beating until potatoes are smooth. Stir in salt and pepper and adjust seasoning. Add more milk, if smoother, thinner potatoes are desired.

Place in 2-quart baking dish and bake until heated through and peaks turn brown, about 30 to 35 minutes. May be refrigerated 2 to 3 days before baking.

Makes 10 servings.

SWEET potatoes are another universal Thanksgiving tradition. Many Texans follow a Southern style and prepare canned yams with lots of butter, brown sugar, cinnamon, marshmallows and pecans. They're called candied yams or sweet potatoes.

CANDIED YAMS (SWEET POTATOES)

1	(29-OUNCE) CAN SWEET POTATOES, DRAINED
1	CUP CHOPPED TOASTED PECANS (omit)
1	CUP BROWN SUGAR, PACKED
4	TABLESPOONS BUTTER, MELTED
1	CUP MINI-MARSHMALLOWS

or 9" square

Preheat oven to 325°–350°. Lightly grease a 13 x 9-inch baking dish. Arrange sweet potatoes in bottom of dish. Sprinkle with pecans, brown sugar, butter, and marshmallows. Bake for 20 to 30 minutes until marshmallows are golden around edges.

Makes 8 to 10 servings.

Mash potatoes with a potato masher. Mix potatoes, sugar + butter.

THIS version of sweet potatoes lets more of the naturally sweet flavor come through without so much gilding of the lily, to use an old Texas phrase. Roasting the potatoes, instead of boiling, caramelizes them and gives them a richer flavor.

MASHED SWEET POTATOES

6	(ABOUT 3 POUNDS) SWEET POTATOES
1	CUP BROWN SUGAR
4	TABLESPOONS BUTTER
2	TABLESPOONS BOURBON OR BRANDY
1	TEASPOON SALT, OR TO TASTE

Preheat oven to 450°. Lightly butter a 2-quart baking dish. Pierce sweet potatoes several times with a fork. Place in oven directly on rack and bake for 1 to 1½ hours or until they yield easily to the touch. Remove from oven and allow to cool slightly. Using oven mitts, cut sweet potatoes in half and scoop out pulp into a large mixing bowl.

Mash sweet potatoes using a potato masher or electric beater. Reserve 2 tablespoons brown sugar. Mix in remaining brown sugar, butter, bourbon or brandy and salt, beating until potatoes are smooth. Spoon sweet potatoes into casserole dish.

Dish may be refrigerated at this point for 2 to 3 days before finishing.

Preheat oven to 325°–350°. Sprinkle remaining 2 tablespoons brown sugar over top of casserole. Bake for 30 to 35 minutes or until heated through.

Makes 10 to 12 servings.

ADD 10 TO 15 MINUTES BAKING TIME TO CASSEROLES THAT HAVE BEEN REFRIGERATED. TO AVOID BREAKING GLASS CASSEROLES, REMOVE FROM REFRIGERATOR 30 MINUTES TO 1 HOUR BEFORE PLACING IN HOT OVEN.

CARL AND REGINA STERLING of Blue Cottage Herb Farm near Kaufman in East Texas shared this idea for holiday carrots several years ago. They serve a similar dish at holiday meals in their farm restaurant.

MINTED CARROTS

1	(16-OUNCE) BAG BABY CARROTS
1	CUP (2 STICKS) BUTTER, MELTED
1	CUP FRESH MINT LEAVES, LIGHTLY PACKED
½	CUP BROWN SUGAR, PACKED
1	TEASPOON SALT, OR TO TASTE

Preheat oven to 325°–350°. Place carrots in a large saucepan with enough cold water to cover. Cook over high heat until water boils. Reduce heat and simmer until carrots are easily pierced with a fork, about 10 to 12 minutes.

Drain carrots and place in a 1½-quart baking dish.

In a blender, combine butter, mint, brown sugar, and salt. Process until smooth and brown sugar dissolves. Pour over carrots and toss to coat vegetables evenly.

Place in oven just until heated through, 15 to 20 minutes. Makes 8 servings.

Variation

Substitute 1 (16-ounce) package frozen green peas, cooked according to package directions, for carrots. Drain peas and rinse in cold water to stop the cooking. Drain again. Return peas to saucepan. In a blender, combine butter, mint, 2 tablespoons granulated sugar (omit brown sugar) and process until smooth and sugar is dissolved. Pour butter mixture over peas and heat through.

ALTHOUGH not a traditional winter vegetable, asparagus has become an anytime option because South American growers can supply it year-round. This simple treatment, laden with sweet and savory flavors, is a refreshing addition to a Thanksgiving table.

ORANGE ASPARAGUS

2	BUNCHES ASPARAGUS
1	TEASPOON SALT, OR TO TASTE
½	CUP BUTTER
2	TABLESPOONS FINELY GRATED ORANGE PEEL
1	CUP ORANGE SECTIONS, CUT INTO ½-INCH PIECES
⅓	CUP GRATED PARMESAN CHEESE OR POMEGRANATE SEEDS

If asparagus have thick, tough stalks, trim ends at point where stalks bend easily. Or, if stalks aren't too tough, simply trim the cut end and peel the bottom inch or so of the stalk using a potato peeler.

Cut asparagus into 1-inch lengths, starting from the tips. Pour enough water into a 12-inch skillet (not cast iron) to depth of 1 inch. Bring water to a boil over high heat and add asparagus and salt. When water returns to the boil, lower heat and simmer until stalks are easily pierced with a fork, but stalks retain considerable crispness, about 2 to 4 minutes.

Carefully drain asparagus so tips don't break. Rinse in cold water to stop the cooking. Wrap in damp paper towels and store in refrigerator until just before serving.

Melt butter in 12-inch skillet and stir in orange peel. Cook until bubbly. Add asparagus and orange pieces; toss to coat well. Cook just until asparagus are heated through.

Sprinkle with Parmesan cheese or pomegranate seeds just before serving.

Makes 8 servings.

NOTHING SEEMS MORE TEDIOUS WHEN GATHERING INGREDIENTS FOR A RECIPE THAN GRATING A TABLESPOON OR TWO OF CITRUS PEEL. SO GET THIS BASIC PREPARATION OUT OF THE WAY AT ONCE. PEEL AND GRATE PLENTY AHEAD OF TIME SO YOU DON'T HAVE TO SLOW DOWN WHEN COOKING. USE A POTATO PEELER TO SCRAPE OFF STRIPS OF PEEL FROM 2 ORANGES AND 4 LEMONS. DON'T SCRAPE DEEP ENOUGH TO GET THE BITTER WHITE PITH. USE A BLENDER OR MINI-CHOPPER TO PROCESS STRIPS TO A FINE CONSISTENCY OR FINELY CHOP ON A CUTTING BOARD WITH A SHARP KNIFE. STORE ORANGE AND LEMON PEEL SEPARATELY IN RESEALABLE PLASTIC FREEZER BAGS OR RIGID PLASTIC CONTAINERS. GRATED OR CHOPPED PEEL WILL STORE IN THE REFRIGERATOR FOR A WEEK. IT WILL FREEZE FOR A MONTH. USE AS NEEDED FOR THE FLAVOR OF ORANGE OR LEMON WITHOUT THE ACIDITY OF THE JUICE.

LIKE asparagus, zucchini have become a year-round favorite on the produce aisle. Roasting gives them a richer flavor than usual sautéing or steaming methods.

ROASTED ZUCCHINI

2	POUNDS MEDIUM ZUCCHINI, ABOUT 6 SQUASH
2	TABLESPOONS OLIVE OIL
1	TABLESPOON BUTTER
½	CUP THINLY SLICED ONION RINGS
1	TEASPOON SALT, OR TO TASTE
1	TEASPOON PEPPER, OR TO TASTE
1	TEASPOON DRIED THYME, OPTIONAL
¼	CUP GRATED PARMESAN CHEESE

Preheat oven to 325°–350°. Trim ends of zucchini. Cut in half lengthwise. Cut each half into approximately 1½-inch pieces. Arrange zucchini in a single layer in a 9 x 13-inch baking dish.

Heat olive oil in a skillet over medium-high heat. Add onions and cook until onions are soft, about 3 to 4 minutes. Add butter and stir just until butter is melted. Add salt, pepper and thyme, if desired. Spread onions over zucchini pieces. Drizzle any remaining butter/oil mixture over zucchini. Toss to coat zucchini evenly. Add a bit more salt and pepper if desired.

Bake until zucchini and onions begin to brown on the edges, about 30 minutes. Sprinkle with cheese and return to oven just until cheese melts.

Makes 8 servings.

THIS is a traditional Southern touch for Texas holiday tables, from Thanksgiving to Christmas. Basically a fruit salad, ambrosia becomes holiday food with the addition of shredded coconut and mini-marshmallows. A personal note, however: No one in our family likes coconut or mini-marshmallows, so the ambrosia on our table is merely fruit salad.

This recipe is a guideline. Use whatever fruits you like. The recipe calls for fresh, but don't hesitate to use a can or two, depending on what's available and convenient.

TEXAS AMBROSIA (FRUIT SALAD)

1	ORANGE
1	GRAPEFRUIT
1	RED PEAR
1	GREEN PEAR
1	CUP SEEDLESS RED GRAPES
1	CUP SEEDLESS GREEN GRAPES
1	PEELED, CORED, AND SLICED PINEAPPLE, AVAILABLE IN MANY SUPERMARKET PRODUCE SECTIONS
1–2	TABLESPOONS SUGAR
1	POMEGRANATE
1	CUP SHREDDED COCONUT, OPTIONAL
½	CUP TOASTED PECANS, OPTIONAL
1	BANANA
1	TABLESPOON LEMON JUICE
1	CUP MINI-MARSHMALLOWS, OPTIONAL

Peel orange and grapefruit. Be sure to remove the bitter white membrane called pith. Hold fruit over a large bowl while peeling to retain as much of the juice as possible. Slice the fruit into thin rounds. (This is much easier than trying to separate fruit into sections and it looks nicer.)

Core pears, but do not peel. Cut pears into eighths, then into bite-size pieces. Add to bowl and toss with orange and grapefruit slices, mixing well. The citrus juice will inhibit

TEXAS AMBROSIA
(FRUIT SALAD), P. 26

browning. (Apples may also be used, but they are more sus-
ceptible to browning than pears.)

If grapes are quite large, cut them in half; otherwise, add
whole grapes to bowl.

Cut pineapple slices into bite-size pieces and stir into
fruit mixture. Sprinkle sugar over fruit, stir, cover, and let
stand for an hour or refrigerate overnight.

Peel pomegranate and separate seeds. Place in plastic
bag and reserve until serving time.

No more than an hour before serving time, add pomegranate seeds, coconut, and pecans, if desired. Peel and
slice banana. Sprinkle banana slices with lemon juice. Add
banana to salad and toss well to coat with juices to further
inhibit browning. Add marshmallows just before serving.

Makes 10 to 12 servings.

"PUTTING UP" summer's bounty has long been a treasured skill in rural Texas homes. For many Texans, a Thanksgiving feast just wouldn't be the same without something pickled or candied. Of course, there is a wide variety of products available in the supermarket or specialty markets, including the fine New Canaan brand from the Texas Hill Country. Their pickled green beans are particularly notable. Whether bought or homemade, pickled okra, dill pickles, sweet gherkins, bread and butter pickles, pickled peppers, relishes such as chow-chow and watermelon pickles are traditional in many homes and served in Grandmother's cut-glass or crystal dishes made for these specialties.

Pickling is time- and equipment-intensive. The following recipe is a shortcut version for contemporary time and tastes. Ironically, the recipe is adapted from a collection compiled in 1978 by the New Ulm, Texas, Volunteer Firemen's Auxiliary. This small German community, my mother's hometown, lies between Houston and Austin. Now, there's a place where women knew how to ride, bake, and cut up a whole chicken! They didn't take many shortcuts, and the men were darn good barbecue cooks as well.

SHORTCUT SWEET PICKLES

1	(16-OUNCE) JAR WHOLE DILL PICKLES
3	CUPS SUGAR
1–1½	CUPS WHITE VINEGAR
⅓	CUP PICKLING SPICE

Cut pickles into ¼-inch thick rounds. Layer one-third of the pickle slices in the bottom of a 9 x 9-inch glass baking dish. Spread evenly with 1 cup sugar. (Pickle layer and sugar layer should be approximately the same thickness.)

Repeat layers using remaining pickles and sugar, ending with sugar. Let stand until sugar is dissolved, or about 1 hour.

Combine 1 cup vinegar and pickling spice. Pour over pickles. Add more vinegar, if needed, to cover pickles and dissolve any remaining sugar. Cover dish tightly with plastic wrap and refrigerate overnight. Pickles are then ready to eat. For longer storage, place pickles in original jar. Store in refrigerator.

Makes 1 (16-ounce) jar.

TEXAS is a wonderful mixture of ethnic identities. Some have melded to become a Texas tradition; others remain distinct. And depending on one's heritage, the Thanksgiving meal, or other feasts, may require a flavor from the old country.

For Texans with German or Eastern European roots, that could be a platter of steaming sauerkraut and sausage.

SAUSAGE *and* SAUERKRAUT

1	(12-OUNCE) LINK SMOKED POLISH OR GERMAN SAUSAGE
1	CUP THIN SLICES GREEN APPLE, UNPEELED
1	CUP THINLY SLICED ONION
¼	TEASPOON SALT, OR TO TASTE
½	TEASPOON PEPPER, OR TO TASTE
2	TABLESPOONS BROWN SUGAR
4	CUPS SAUERKRAUT
½	CUP BEER, WATER, OR SHERRY

Preheat oven to 325°–350°. Cut sausage into ¼-inch thick slices. Place in skillet over medium heat. Cook until edges are brown, turning on all sides, about 5 minutes. Using a slotted spoon, remove sausage and reserve.

Add apple and onion slices to sausage drippings and cook until soft, about 5 minutes. Season with salt, pepper and brown sugar. Combine seasoned apple and onion with sauerkraut in 2-quart casserole dish. Adjust seasoning to taste.

Arrange sausage over sauerkraut and pour beer, water or sherry over sausage and sauerkraut. Cover and bake for 30 minutes or until heated through.

Note. This is an excellent use for venison sausage. Many a hunter finds a freezerful of sausage at the end of deer season. This is one way to use it up. Serve with mashed potatoes for a full meal.

Makes 8 servings.

TEXANS along the border or in the Western part of the state may serve up a platter of enchiladas alongside the turkey and dressing. They're likely to show up at Christmas and New Year's as well. Like tamales, enchiladas are a three-part production: the sauce, the filling and the assembly. You can shortcut the process by using 3 cans of enchilada sauce instead of making chili gravy.

TEX-MEX ENCHILADAS

Chili Gravy

2	TABLESPOONS SHORTENING
2	TABLESPOONS FLOUR
2	TABLESPOONS CHILI POWDER
3	CUPS WARM WATER, OR 2 CUPS WARM WATER PLUS 1 (8-OUNCE) CAN TOMATO SAUCE
1	TEASPOON SALT, OR TO TASTE
½	TEASPOON PEPPER, OR TO TASTE

Place shortening in skillet over medium heat. When shortening melts, stir in flour, using a whisk or the back of a slotted spoon. Add chili powder, water (and tomato sauce). Allow liquid to simmer, stirring occasionally. Add salt and pepper to taste. Cook until thickened, about 15 to 20 minutes. Set sauce aside.

Filling

¾	POUND GROUND BEEF
¼	TEASPOON SALT, OR TO TASTE
¼	TEASPOON PEPPER, OR TO TASTE

Place ground beef in small skillet and cook over medium heat until meat is browned. Season with salt and pepper. Drain well and set aside.

Assembly

4	CUPS GRATED LONGHORN OR CHEDDAR CHEESE
1	CUP FINELY CHOPPED ONION
12	CORN TORTILLAS
2	TABLESPOONS COOKING OIL

Preheat oven to 350°. Lightly coat a 9 x 13-inch glass baking dish with non-stick cooking spray.

Ready the ingredients in assembly-line fashion; chili gravy, beef, cheese, and onions.

Place cooking oil in small skillet over medium heat. Dip a tortilla in hot oil until softened, about 15 seconds. Allow excess grease to drain back into skillet. Dip tortilla in chili gravy and place the tortilla in the pan.

Add 1 to 2 tablespoons of ground beef, 1 to 2 tablespoons cheese, and 1 to 2 teaspoons chopped onion down the middle of the tortilla. Roll tortilla to enclose filling and place seam side down in the pan.

Continue filling and rolling to make 12 tortillas. Arrange tortillas to fit snugly in pan. Pour chili gravy over tortillas and sprinkle with remaining cheese and onion. Bake until bubbly, 15 to 20 minutes.

Makes 12 enchiladas, 4 to 6 servings.

Note. For cheese enchiladas, omit ground beef. Use cheese and onions as filling.

IN many Hispanic households, no holiday is complete without a day or two of tamale-making. This is a time for one generation to pass along family traditions to the next. It is a time for much merrymaking, laughter, some stories, perhaps a confession or two and even a few tears.

Of course, there are Mexican restaurants and taquerias in most Texas cities where tamales can be purchased or special ordered. Many supermarkets even offer several varieties, both canned and frozen. But tamales, more than many other foods, are best seasoned by togetherness.

Allow two days (or one very long day) for tamale-making. The filling improves when refrigerated overnight.

Tamale-making is a three-stage process: cooking the filling, mixing the dough, and wrapping/steaming.

TEX-MEX HOT TAMALES

Filling

3	POUNDS LEAN, BONELESS PORK ROAST, OR 2 POUNDS PORK PLUS 1 POUND BONELESS VENISON
8	CUPS WATER, OR MORE AS NEEDED
2	CUPS CHOPPED ONION
4	CLOVES GARLIC, CRUSHED
2	TEASPOONS SALT, OR TO TASTE
2	TEASPOONS PEPPER, OR TO TASTE
1	(14.5-OUNCE) CAN ENCHILADA SAUCE OR 1 (15-OUNCE) CAN TOMATO SAUCE PLUS 1 TABLESPOON CHILI POWDER
1–2	TEASPOONS SUGAR, OR TO TASTE, OPTIONAL

Cut pork (and venison) into 2- to 3-inch chunks and place in a large, heavy saucepan, Dutch oven, or stockpot. Add enough water to just cover meat. Bring liquid to a boil over high heat. Reduce heat to simmer. Skim any foam that accumulates.

Add onion, garlic, salt, and pepper. Cover pot and cook over low heat for 2 to 3 hours, until meat is very tender and falling apart, adding more water if necessary to maintain level. Strain cooking liquid and reserve.

Cool meat enough to handle. Finely shred meat with fingers or use two forks to pull it into thin strips, going with the grain of the meat. Chopping does not produce the proper consistency.

Place meat in mixing bowl and add enchilada sauce or tomato sauce and chili powder. Add enough reserved stock (about 1 cup) to coat the meat with sauce. Mixture should not be watery; adjust liquid as necessary. Mix well and adjust seasoning with salt, pepper, and sugar. Cover and refrigerate overnight or chill several hours. Reserve and refrigerate any remaining broth for use in the dough.

HISPANIC GROCERIES AND SUPERMARKETS WITH A LARGE SELECTION OF ETHNIC FOODS SELL READY-MADE TAMALE DOUGH IN THE REFRIGERATOR OR FREEZER CASE. BUYING PREPARED DOUGH WILL SHORTCUT THE TAMALE-MAKING PROCESS SOMEWHAT WITHOUT SACRIFICING THE RITUAL.

Dough

10 CUPS MASA HARINA (FOUND ALONGSIDE FLOUR AND CORNMEAL IN THE SUPERMARKET)

3–4 TEASPOONS SALT, OR TO TASTE

2 TEASPOONS BAKING POWDER

2 CUPS LARD (NO SUBSTITUTES)

3 CUPS RESERVED PORK STOCK, HEATED (USE CHICKEN STOCK IF MORE LIQUID IS NEEDED)

Combine masa harina, salt, and baking powder; set aside. Place lard in a large mixing bowl and beat at high speed with an electric beater until light and fluffy, about 3 to 5 minutes. Add masa mixture in 3 to 4 batches, alternately with the warm (not hot) broth, beating constantly.

TEX-MEX HOT TAMALES, P. 32

Dough should be soft, but pliable, not watery. To test it, place a small piece of dough in a cup of water. If it floats, it is the right consistency.

Wrapping and Steaming

60 DRIED CORN HUSKS

HOT WATER

Several hours before preparing dough, rinse husks and remove any silk. Soak in hot water for several hours to soften.

To Shape and Wrap Tamales

Pat dry the corn husks. Ready the dough and filling in assembly-line fashion. Wet your hands. Place a husk in the palm of one hand, and using the back of a spoon, spread about 2 tablespoons of the dough into a rectangle, starting at the wide end of the shuck. Leave about 1½ inches at the wide end of the shuck, about 3 inches at the pointed end. Spread dough to within ¾ inch of the sides. Spread 1 to 2 tablespoons tamale filling lengthwise down the center of the dough. Roll sides of tamales to seal the filling. Fold over wide end to seal bottom. Place folded side down on cookie sheet or large sheet of foil. Repeat until dough and filling are used. You should have about 4 dozen.

To Steam

Use a large tamale steamer or large pot with a rack or colander in the bottom. Fill bottom with water to depth of about 1 inch. Water should not touch the rack. Line rack with some of the remaining shucks. Arrange tamales vertically—wide, folded end down—on rack. Tamales should be packed, but not crammed, so that they will remain vertical. Cover the tamales with more corn husks or a layer of clean dish towels to prevent the tamales from absorbing too much water. They should be steamed, not immersed. Place lid on pot.

Bring water to a boil, reduce heat, and simmer for 1½ hours. Make sure water does not cook away during this time; add more as needed. Check tamales for doneness. Tamales are done when the masa easily separates from the husk and the tamale retains its shape. If not done, continue steaming for up to 3 hours or as needed.

If necessary, cook tamales in batches, reserving tamales in refrigerator until ready to steam.

Cooked tamales may be refrigerated several days or frozen for several weeks. Reheat, tightly wrapped in foil, in a 300° oven, about 30 minutes.

Makes about 4 dozen.

I'M THE ONE THAT BRINGS THE TAMALES TO MY WIFE'S FAMILY'S HOUSE. TAMALES WERE ALWAYS ON MY FAMILY'S THANKSGIVING, CHRISTMAS, AND NEW YEAR'S TABLE. I USUALLY BUY THEM THESE DAYS, BUT IT JUST WOULDN'T BE THE SAME WITH-OUT TAMALES. MY SISTERS OR AUNTS USED TO MAKE THEM. THE WOMEN WOULD GATHER IN THE KITCHEN AND COOK AND GOSSIP. BACK THEN, THE MEN JUST SAT ON THE PORCH AND TALKED.

Juan Garcia

FOR many African-Americans, macaroni and cheese is traditional on a feasting table. Everybody's momma makes "the best." This is a streamlined version of old-fashioned macaroni and cheese. Not as easy as the boxed or frozen varieties, it is simpler than the classic version calling for a "scratch" cheese sauce. It'll do any momma proud.

MACARONI AND CHEESE, TURNIP GREENS, PUR-
PLE HULL PEAS, AND CANDIED YAMS ARE STAN-
DARD ON OUR THANKSGIVING TABLE. AND, YOU
KNOW, THE SECRET TO GOOD DRESSING IS A RICH
BROTH. SEASON IT REAL WELL AND USE TURKEY
DRIPPINGS. MIX THAT IN WITH THE INGREDIENTS
FOR THE DRESSING—THE CORNBREAD, VEGETA-
BLES AND SOME EGGS. WHILE ALL THAT COOKS,
I'M THINKING THAT IN A FEW HOURS I'LL BE ABLE
TO WRAP MY MOUTH AROUND ALL THOSE FLAVORS.

Smokey John Reaves

MACARONI AND CHEESE, P. 37

MACARONI *and* CHEESE

½	POUND MACARONI OR OTHER DRY PASTA
1	TABLESPOON BUTTER
1	TEASPOON YELLOW MUSTARD
1	EGG, LIGHTLY BEATEN
½	TEASPOON SALT
3	CUPS (ABOUT 12 OUNCES) GRATED CHEDDAR OR OTHER YELLOW CHEESE (DIVIDED USE)
1	TABLESPOON FLOUR
1½	CUPS MILK

Preheat oven to 325°–350°. Grease a 1½-quart casserole.

Cook macaroni in large saucepan according to package directions. Pasta should be tender, but not too soft. Drain well and allow to cool slightly. Return to saucepan.

Stir in butter, mustard, egg, and salt. Add 2½ cups cheese and flour, tossing well to evenly distribute ingredients. Turn mixture into prepared casserole dish. Pour milk over macaroni and cheese. Use the back of a spoon to press down ingredients and level the top. Bake for about 35 minutes. Sprinkle remaining cheese on top and bake about 10 minutes longer or until the custard is set and the top is golden and crusty.

Makes 8 servings.

OF course, the easiest crust of all is cut and rolled for you, available in the refrigerator case at the supermarket. And there's absolutely no shame in using one.

But if you want to try your hand at pastry, try this easy crust: simple to assemble and forgiving to work with. Not as flaky as a crust with butter or shortening, it nevertheless brings homemade crust within the reach of even a beginner.

EASY PIE CRUST

1¼	CUPS SIFTED FLOUR (SIFT BEFORE MEASURING)
¼	TEASPOON SALT
¼	CUP MILK
⅓	CUP VEGETABLE OIL

Stir together flour and salt. Combine milk and oil; add all at once to flour. Using a fork, then your hands, combine flour and liquid to form a ball of dough. Flatten to a disk about 6 inches in diameter.

Press into a 9-inch pie plate, covering bottom and up the sides evenly. Crust should overlap edge of pan about ½ inch. Turn crust under and shape edge of crust using fingers to create a fluted or pleated edge.

An alternate technique: Place dough between two sheets of waxed paper. Roll the dough about 2 inches larger than the diameter of the pan. Remove top sheet of wax paper. Gently place pan in center of dough and, using edges of waxed paper, turn over pan and dough to release dough into pie pan. Gently ease dough into pan to fit the sides. Proceed as above.

Fill and bake as directed in pie recipe.

For a baked or "blind" crust, prick bottom and sides of crust with a fork. Place crust in 450° oven for 10 minutes or just until crust is set and begins to take on a golden cast. Cool before filling.

Makes 1 (9-inch) crust.

THE following is a classic pastry. It works best with the premeasured shortening, the kind that comes in wrapped sticks, like butter. Lighter and fluffier, the shortening makes a flakier crust, similar to one made with lard, but without the cholesterol.

BASIC PIE CRUST

3	CUPS SIFTED FLOUR (SIFT BEFORE MEASURING)
1	TEASPOON SALT
1¼	CUPS SHORTENING (PREFERABLY PRE-MEASURED IN STICKS)
8–10	TABLESPOONS COLD WATER

Sift together the flour and salt; using a pastry cutter, two knives or fingers, blend shortening and flour together until mixture is crumbly.

Stir in cold water, adding just enough for pastry to hold together, so that pastry forms a smooth ball.

If using a food processor, combine flour, salt, and shortening in work bowl. Process on-and-off several times until mixture is crumbly.

With motor running, add liquid in a steady stream and process just until mixture forms a ball.

Refrigerate an hour for easier handling. Divide dough and roll out on a lightly floured board to make pastry for a (9-inch) two-crust pie or two (9-inch) crusts. Roll the dough about 2 inches larger than the diameter of the pan. Drape crust over the rolling pin and ease it into pan, fitting it against bottom and sides. Crust should overlap edge of pan about ½ inch. Turn crust under and shape edge using fingers to create a fluted or pleated edge.

Fill and bake as directed in pie recipe.

For a baked or "blind" crust, prick bottom and sides of crust with a fork. Place crust in 450° oven for 10 minutes or just until crust is set and begins to take on a golden cast. Cool before filling.

PECANS are a favorite all over Texas and you can find them in just about every course of a Texas holiday feast, from beginning to end. But these native nuts show best in a pie. Add a scoop of vanilla ice cream or a dollop of whipped cream and you've got a dessert to die for.

This pecan pie is heavy on filling and nuts. Some pies go light on the filling so the pie is dense with nuts. I've always thought the custard was as good as the nuts.

> **HOLIDAYS IN TEXAS EVOKE AN EXCITEMENT IN MY BODY AND SOUL. I NOURISH MYSELF WITH FEAST, FESTIVITY, FELLOWSHIP, FLAVOR, FAMILY, FATHER, AND NEW FOCUS. LONG LIVE THE TEXAS FOODS OF THE HOLIDAYS!**
>
> *Susan Teepler Auler*

PECAN PIE

½	CUP SUGAR
½	CUP UNSALTED BUTTER
¼	TEASPOON SALT
1	CUP WHITE OR DARK CORN SYRUP
3	EGGS, BEATEN UNTIL FOAMY
2	TEASPOONS VANILLA
2	CUPS COARSELY CHOPPED PECANS OR
	1 CUP COARSELY CHOPPED PECANS AND
	½ CUP PECAN HALVES
1	UNBAKED (9-INCH) PIE SHELL, REFRIGERATED

Preheat oven to 350°. Combine sugar, salt, and corn syrup in a small saucepan over medium heat. (Light or dark corn syrup will do. The flavor and color of the filling will be more intense and darker with dark corn syrup.) Cook until sugar dissolves and mixture is hot. Stir in butter and remove from heat.

Stir until butter melts and liquid cools slightly. Add eggs, vanilla, and chopped pecans. Pour into chilled pie shell and smooth filling evenly. If using pecan halves, arrange in concentric circles starting at outer edge of pie.

Make a ring out of aluminum foil to shield the crust. Place over crust. Place pie in oven and bake for about 45 to 50 minutes or until a knife inserted in the filling comes out clean.

Serve warm with ice cream or at room temperature with a dollop of whipped cream.

Note. Although a pecan pie with beautifully arranged halves on the top looks pretty, it is more difficult to cut and eat. Nicely chopped nuts make slicing easier.

Makes 8 servings.

Pumpkin Pie

1	CUP CANNED PUMPKIN
1	CUP EVAPORATED (NOT SWEETENED CONDENSED) MILK
1	CUP LIGHT BROWN SUGAR, FIRMLY PACKED
3	EGGS, LIGHTLY BEATEN
¼	CUP BOURBON OR BRANDY
1	TEASPOON PUMPKIN PIE SPICE (OR ½ TEASPOON NUTMEG, ½ TEASPOON GINGER, ¼ TEASPOON MACE)
1	TEASPOON CINNAMON
½	TEASPOON SALT
1	(9-INCH) PIE SHELL, UNBAKED

Combine pumpkin, evaporated milk, and sugar in medium bowl, beating at low speed with electric mixer. Blend until sugar is dissolved and mixture is smooth. Stir in eggs, bourbon, spice, and salt. Mix well.

Pour filling into prepared pie shell. Bake for 50 to 55 minutes or until tip of a sharp knife inserted in center comes out clean. Cool on wire rack.

Makes 8 servings.

Sweet Potato Pie

2	CUPS CANNED YAMS OR SWEET POTATOES, DRAINED AND MASHED
2	EGGS, WELL-BEATEN
¾	CUP MILK
¼	CUP BUTTER, MELTED
1	CUP SUGAR
1	TEASPOON CINNAMON
1	TEASPOON VANILLA
¼	TEASPOON SALT
1	(9-INCH) PIE SHELL, UNBAKED

Preheat oven to 350°. In a large bowl, combine mashed sweet potatoes, eggs, milk and butter, mixing well. Stir in sugar, cinnamon, vanilla, and salt. Pour into pie shell and bake for 55 minutes to 1 hour, or until tip of a sharp knife inserted in center comes out clean. Cool on wire rack.

Makes 8 servings.

HANUKKAH

Hanukkah Menu

CHOPPED LIVER, 45
 WITH RYE OR
 PUMPERNICKEL BREAD
 ROUNDS

BRISKET POT ROAST
 WITH VEGETABLES AND
 GRAVY, 47

LATKES
 (POTATO PANCAKES), 49
 WITH APPLESAUCE, 51

NON-DAIRY KUGEL, 53

FRESH SPINACH SALAD WITH
 TEXAS GRAPEFRUIT, 85

MACAROONS, 58

SUGAR COOKIES, 93
 (OMIT DAIRY PRODUCTS)

Dairy Hanukkah Menu

LATKES (POTATO PANCAKES)
 WITH SOUR CREAM, 49

DAIRY PLATE FROM FAVORITE
 DELI (EGG SALAD, TUNA
 SALAD, HERRING IN SOUR
 CREAM, ETC.)

TEXAS AMBROSIA
 (FRUIT SALAD), 26

SUFGANIYOT
 (JELLY DOUGHNUTS), 54

SWEET NOODLE KUGEL, 52

CHOCOLATE CHESS PIE, 113

TRADITIONALLY, Hanukkah is one of the less serious Jewish holidays, although in recent years it has come to be celebrated with more festivity because it falls during that happy, busy time between Thanksgiving and New Year's. The eight-day Festival of Lights commemorates the expulsion of the Syrians by the Maccabees in 165 B.C. Specifically, it celebrates the miracle of a single vessel of consecrated oil, barely enough for one day, that burned for eight days. It also celebrates the rededication of the Temple in Jerusalem. This holiday is symbolized by the lighting of candles, one for each night of the celebration, on the menorah, a nine-branched candlestick. The middle candle serves to light the others. Foods fried in oil are also symbolic of the holiday, particularly latkes (potato pancakes) and jelly doughnuts.

It is a fun holiday, particularly for children, who receive gifts each night of the celebration. The dreidel, a top, is spun for wagering, similar to the throwing of dice. Gelt, chocolate wrapped in gold foil to look like coins, is the currency of Hanukkah.

Jewish dietary laws forbid serving dairy and meat at the same meal. Therefore, a Hanukkah menu with brisket would include latkes garnished with applesauce. Recipes that call for butter may be made using margarine as a substitute, but other dairy products, such as sour cream, cream cheese, or milk, are forbidden.

A dairy meal for Hanukkah might consist of a variety of salads, such as tuna or chopped egg, various marinated fish dishes and spreads, perhaps a pasta or kugel (a noodle casserole), as well as latkes and sour cream. Jewish-style delis offer "dairy plates," a selection of dishes that adhere to Jewish tradition and dietary law.

THE TEXAS HOLIDAY COOKBOOK

CHOPPED liver is the punch line of many a Yiddish joke. It is also the beginning of many a holiday meal. Sally Bernstein, an Austin cooking teacher, likes this version.

CHOPPED LIVER

1	POUND CALF'S LIVER
4	HARD-COOKED EGGS, CHOPPED
3	SLICES WHITE BREAD, CRUSTS REMOVED
1	TEASPOON SALT, OR TO TASTE
1	TEASPOON PEPPER, OR TO TASTE
2–3	TABLESPOONS CHICKEN FAT OR COOKING OIL, MORE OR LESS AS NEEDED
¼	CUP FINELY CHOPPED ONION, OPTIONAL

Preheat oven to 350°. Line a baking sheet with foil. Place liver on foil and bake for about 5 minutes. Turn and bake until cooked through, a total of 10 to 15 minutes. Juices should run clear.

Pull off skin; discard. Cut liver into chunks and chop fine. Add hard-cooked eggs.

Place bread in just enough water to cover until it has absorbed all it can. Squeeze out excess moisture and crumble bread into liver mixture. Add just enough fat or oil to make the mixture soft and workable. Add salt and pepper; adjust seasoning to taste. Stir in onion, if desired.

Chill and serve cold as a spread for rye or pumpernickel bread rounds.

Makes 10 to 12 servings.

SHORTCUT. CUT LIVER INTO CHUNKS AND PLACE IN WORK BOWL OF FOOD PROCESSOR FITTED WITH CHOPPING BLADE. PULSE ON-AND-OFF TO CHOP TO DESIRED CONSISTENCY. ADD BREAD, THEN OIL AND PROCESS TO DESIRED CONSISTENCY. FOLD IN EGGS, SALT, PEPPER, AND ONION.

THESE meatballs are a favorite party appetizer in Texas homes throughout the holidays. Sally Bernstein's version is great on an hors d'oeuvres buffet.

SWEET *and* SOUR MEATBALLS

1	(12-OUNCE) BOTTLE CHILI SAUCE
1	(16-OUNCE) CAN JELLIED CRANBERRY SAUCE
¼	CUP BREAD CRUMBS
3	EGGS
3	POUNDS GROUND BEEF
2	TEASPOONS SALT, OR TO TASTE
1	TEASPOON PEPPER, OR TO TASTE
3	TABLESPOONS MUSTARD
5	TABLESPOONS KETCHUP
1	CUP WATER

Combine chili sauce and cranberry sauce in a large, heavy saucepan over medium heat. Bring to a boil, lower heat, and allow to simmer while shaping meatballs.

Place ground beef, bread crumbs, eggs, mustard, ketchup, salt and pepper in a large bowl. Using a wooden spoon and/or hands, mix well to evenly distribute ingredients. Add water to loosen mixture for easier mixing.

Form meatballs, about 1 inch in diameter. Add to simmering sauce mixture and cook slowly for 2 to 3 hours.

Serve hot in a chafing dish or slow cooker.

Makes about 25 to 30 meatballs.

Pot roast has come to be a favorite most common main course for Hanukkah and brisket is the meat of choice.

BRISKET POT ROAST *with* VEGETABLES

1	(4–5-POUND) BEEF BRISKET, TRIMMED OF FAT
	NON-STICK COOKING SPRAY
2	TEASPOONS SALT, OR TO TASTE
2	TEASPOONS BLACK PEPPER, OR TO TASTE
2	CUPS THINLY SLICED ONION RINGS, ABOUT 1 LARGE ONION
2	CLOVES GARLIC, CRUSHED
1	CUP WATER OR ½ CUP WATER PLUS ½ CUP DRY RED WINE
1	(8-OUNCE) CAN TOMATO SAUCE
8	MEDIUM RED POTATOES (ABOUT 2 POUNDS)
1	(8-OUNCE) PACKAGE BABY CARROTS
1–2	TABLESPOONS INSTANT DISSOLVING FLOUR, OPTIONAL

Rinse brisket and pat dry. Rub brisket on all sides with salt and pepper. Coat a Dutch oven with non-stick cooking spray and heat over medium-high heat. Add brisket and cook until brown on all sides, turning as needed.

Remove meat to a large platter to catch any juices. Cook sliced onions in pan drippings over medium-high heat until well-browned and caramelized, about 10 minutes. Add a tablespoon of oil, if needed. Remove onions from pan and reserve.

Place brisket and any accumulated juices in pan and layer onions on top and all around.

Preheat oven to 300°.

Stir together water (or water and wine) and tomato sauce. Pour over brisket. Bring liquid to a boil over medium-high heat.

When liquid boils, cover pot with lid and place pot in oven. Cook for 3 to 4 hours until brisket is tender. Check occasionally and add more water if the liquid evaporates.

FOR BEST RESULTS, USE A FLAT CUT OR "FIRST CUT" BRISKET. THIS CUT ELIMINATES A FATTY FLAP THAT CAN MAKE FOR VERY GREASY GRAVY. BE SURE YOU BUY A TRIMMED BRISKET, UNLIKE FOR BARBECUE WHEN AN UNTRIMMED BRISKET IS PREFERABLE.

When brisket is tender, remove the pan from the oven. Transfer brisket to a large platter, cover with foil and keep warm, reserving cooking liquid from roast.

Cut potatoes into quarters. Place carrots and potatoes in pot roast liquid and simmer over low heat, covered, about 15 minutes until potatoes and carrots can be pierced easily with a fork.

Adjust seasoning with salt and pepper. If a thicker gravy is desired, sprinkle instant dissolving flour into gravy, stirring constantly. Cook over low heat just until thickened. Remove from heat and keep warm.

Slice brisket against the grain ¼- to ½-inch thick. Serve brisket with potatoes, carrots and plenty of gravy.

Makes 8 to 10 servings.

Variation

For a sweet and sour style pot roast, add 2 tablespoons packed brown sugar and ¼ cup apple cider vinegar to cooking liquid. Omit red wine.

> THERE SEEMS TO BE LITTLE IN THE WAY OF "TRADITIONAL FOODS" (FOR HANUKKAH) LIKE THOSE AT PASSOVER OR NEW YEAR. EXCEPT FOR THE LATKES. THE JELLY DOUGHNUTS ARE BECOMING QUITE POPULAR, TOO.
>
> *Kyra Effren*

LATKES, more like hash brown potatoes than pancakes, may be served with sour cream or applesauce, depending on the rest of the menu.

A great latke is brown and crisp on the outside—white, soft, and steaming on the inside. The flavor and texture of a hot latke plays equally well against the cool of sour cream or applesauce. The former offers tart, creamy contrast, while the latter provides the palate with smooth, sweet refreshment.

Potato Latkes (Pancakes)

8   CUPS GRATED RUSSET POTATOES
    (PEELED), ABOUT 4 LARGE
1   CUP GRATED ONION, ABOUT 1 MEDIUM
2   EGGS, LIGHTLY BEATEN (ADD 1 OR 2
    MORE AS NEEDED TO BIND THE BATTER)
4   TABLESPOONS MATZO MEAL OR FLOUR
1   TEASPOON SALT, OR TO TASTE
½   TEASPOON PEPPER, OR TO TASTE
    OIL FOR FRYING

Peel potatoes and place in a bowl of cold water to prevent discoloration. Using a hand grater, coarsely grate potatoes and onions. As you grate each potato, transfer the shreds to a large colander to drain excess liquid. Add onion to colander. Using your hands, toss potatoes to combine with onions. Using your fingers, squeeze handfuls of potatoes or press potatoes into bottom and sides of colander to release excess liquid. Transfer drained potato and onion mixture to a large mixing bowl.

Add eggs, matzo or flour, salt, and pepper, mixing well to distribute ingredients and coat potatoes. Allow batter to rest for about 10 minutes.

Heat ¼-inch oil to 375°–400° in a large skillet. When oil is hot, but not smoking, drop batter by tablespoonfuls into hot oil. Batter will spread, but use the back of a spoon to flatten pancake, if needed, for uniform thickness. Do not crowd the pan; the sides of pancakes should not touch.

Cook until brown on one side, about 4 minutes. Turn and brown other side, another 3 to 4 minutes. Drain on paper towels and keep warm while frying remaining batter. Serve immediately with sour cream or applesauce.

Makes 8 servings, about 24 latkes.

SHORTCUTS

- FIT FOOD PROCESSOR WITH COARSE SHREDDING DISK. FEED POTATOES THROUGH TUBE, EMPTYING WORK BOWL INTO A LARGE COLANDER AFTER EACH POTATO IS SHREDDED. WHEN ALL POTATOES ARE SHREDDED AND DRAINING, REMOVE SHREDDING DISK AND ATTACH BLADE. CHOP ONION, USING ON-OFF PULSES. PLACE CHOPPED ONION IN COLANDER WITH POTATOES. PROCEED AS ABOVE.

- INSTEAD OF GRATING FRESH POTATOES, USE 2 (1-POUND, 4-OUNCE) PACKAGES SHREDDED POTATOES, THE KIND FOUND IN THE DAIRY CASE. ADD 1 OR 2 ADDITIONAL EGGS TO BIND THE POTATOES AND PROCEED AS ABOVE.

LATKES MAY BE MADE AHEAD AND FROZEN. ARRANGE LATKES IN A SINGLE LAYER ON COOKIE SHEETS AND PLACE IN FREEZER. WHEN LATKES ARE FROZEN SOLID, PLACE THEM IN A FREEZER BAG. REHEAT IN A PREHEATED 400° OVEN. PLACE FROZEN LATKES IN A SINGLE LAYER ON COOKIE SHEET. HEAT UNTIL SIZZLING, ABOUT 10 TO 15 MINUTES.

THIS variation, developed by Kyra Effren, uses sweet potatoes, definitely a Southern adaptation of the traditional Jewish favorite.

KYRA'S SWEET POTATO LATKES

3	LARGE SWEET POTATOES, ABOUT 2 POUNDS
2	ONIONS, CHOPPED FINE
2	TABLESPOONS FLOUR
2	TABLESPOONS ROLLED OATS (UNCOOKED OATMEAL)
3	EGGS, LIGHTLY BEATEN
1	TEASPOON SALT, OR TO TASTE
¼	TEASPOON WHITE PEPPER, OR TO TASTE
	OIL FOR FRYING

SOME COOKS LIKE TO PLACE SHREDDED POTATOES IN A DOUBLE THICKNESS OF CHEESECLOTH OR A COARSE DISH TOWEL AND SQUEEZE TO REMOVE EXCESS MOISTURE. DON'T FRET IF THE POTATOES TURN PINK, THEN START TO BROWN. THIS HAPPENS WHEN THEY ARE EXPOSED TO AIR. WHEN COOKED, HOWEVER, THEY TURN A LOVELY WHITE-POTATO COLOR AGAIN. YOU DO WANT TO WORK FAST ENOUGH, HOWEVER, TO PREVENT THEM FROM TURNING THE NEXT SHADE, A DINGY GRAY COLOR. IT WON'T HURT YOU, BUT THAT COLOR DOESN'T COOK AWAY.

Peel the sweet potatoes and finely grate them. In large bowl, combine grated sweet potatoes, onions, flour, oats, eggs, salt, and pepper.

In a heavy-bottomed skillet, heat 1-inch oil over medium-high heat to 375°. Drop latkes by tablespoonfuls into the hot oil, flattening with the back of a spoon. Cook until brown on one side; turn and cook until brown.

Add more oil if needed during cooking. Repeat until all batter is used. Drain fried latkes on absorbent paper towels and keep warm until serving time.

Makes 8 servings.

LATKES ARE THE THING FOR HANUKKAH. YOU'VE GOT TO HAVE LATKES, THE POTATO PAN-CAKES, FOR THE CHILDREN. THE HOLIDAY WOULDN'T BE THE SAME WITHOUT THEM.

Sally Bernstein

El Paso-born Elaine Corn makes this special version of applesauce. She recommends using just about any apple. You'll get great applesauce from Granny Smith, Fuji, Jonathan, Golden Delicious, Macintosh, Rome, or any combination. Red Delicious "is probably the least delicious in the entire apple kingdom," she warns. Her flavor enhancers—vanilla "to make it more like a pie" and butter "to make it rich"—take this applesauce to a new level.

ELAINE'S APPLESAUCE

4	POUNDS (ABOUT 12) APPLES OF ANY VARIETY, TO MAKE ABOUT 8 CUPS CHOPPED
¼	CUP HONEY OR SUGAR, OR A COMBINATION
2	(2-INCH) PIECES CINNAMON STICK
8	WHOLE CLOVES (OR ½ TEASPOON POWDERED CLOVES)
¾–1	CUP WATER
	A PINCH OF FRESHLY GRATED NUTMEG
¼	TEASPOON POWDERED GINGER, OPTIONAL
	JUICE AND FINELY GRATED PEEL FROM 1 LEMON OR 1 ORANGE, OR A COMBINATION
2	TABLESPOONS BUTTER
1–2	TEASPOONS VANILLA, OR TO TASTE

Peel, core, and coarsely chop the apples. Combine apples, honey or sugar, cinnamon, and cloves in a large saucepan over low heat. Add just enough water to create a syrup to coat the fruit. Add a bit less water when using honey.

When liquid begins to bubble, reduce heat and simmer for about 40 minutes. Stir to coat the apples with the pan juices, then occasionally to prevent scorching. The apples will cook down to about half their original volume and become very soft.

Remove cinnamon stick and whole cloves. If a smooth applesauce is desired, process directly in the pot with an immersible blender until very smooth, or process in batches until smooth in a blender. Do not process if a chunky apple-sauce is desired.

Reheat applesauce over low heat, adding nutmeg, ginger, lemon or orange juice and grated peel. Simmer until heated through. Remove from heat and stir in butter and vanilla to taste.

Elaine uses an immersible blender (Braun is one brand) to make this an easy one-pot job. But any blender will do. So will a food processor.

Makes 10 to 12 servings.

KUGELS, noodle or potato puddings, can be sweet with fruit or savory with onion, with or without dairy. Non-dairy kugels are served as side dishes with meat meals. Dairy kugels, sweet or savory, may be served as meatless entrées or side dishes, like macaroni and cheese, or as desserts. Traditional for holiday meals, kugels are as varied as the families who make them. Here are several varieties.

SWEET NOODLE KUGEL

8	OUNCES WIDE EGG NOODLES
1	(8-OUNCE) PACKAGE CREAM CHEESE, SOFTENED, OR COTTAGE CHEESE
½	CUP BUTTER, SOFTENED
4	EGGS
1	CUP MILK
¾	CUP SUGAR
1	TEASPOON VANILLA
2	CUPS CORN FLAKES, OPTIONAL
1	TEASPOON CINNAMON OR NUTMEG

Preheat oven to 350°. Grease or butter a 9 x 13-inch glass baking dish or two 8 x 8-inch baking dishes.

Cook noodles according to package directions. Drain noodles and set aside.

In a medium bowl, combine cream cheese or cottage cheese, butter, eggs, milk, sugar, and vanilla. Using an electric mixer, beat on medium speed until mixture is well-blended and smooth.

Pour cheese mixture over noodles. If desired, top with corn flakes. Sprinkle with cinnamon or nutmeg. Bake for 45 minutes or until golden on top and custard is set.

Variation

For a savory kugel, substitute 2 cups sour cream for milk and stir in 1 teaspoon salt or to taste and 1 teaspoon pepper. Omit sugar and vanilla; corn flakes are optional. Sprinkle with nutmeg.

POTATO KUGEL

8	CUPS GRATED RUSSET POTATO (PEELED), ABOUT 4 LARGE
1	CUP GRATED ONION, ABOUT 1 MEDIUM
4	EGGS, LIGHTLY BEATEN
1	TEASPOON SALT, OR TO TASTE
1	TEASPOON PEPPER, OR TO TASTE
5–6	TABLESPOONS VEGETABLE OIL OR CHICKEN FAT

Brush a 9 x 13-inch glass baking dish with oil or spray generously with non-stick spray. Preheat oven to 350°.

Peel potatoes and place in a bowl of cold water to prevent discoloration. Using a hand grater, coarsely grate potatoes and onions into a large mixing bowl.

Stir in eggs, salt, pepper, and oil. Mix well to coat potato shreds and stop discoloration. Work quickly.

Pour into prepared dish and bake for approximately 1 hour. Raise oven temperature to 450° and bake 5 to 10 minutes longer, or until top is browned.

Makes 8 to 10 servings.

Variation

Cook 16-ounces dry noodles according to package directions. Substitute for grated potato and prepare as above.

If desired, sprinkle with 1 cup crushed cornflakes before baking.

FOR THE TRUE FLAVOR OF JEWISH CUISINE, USE SCHMALTZ, THAT'S CHICKEN FAT, INSTEAD OF VEGETABLE OIL. OF COURSE, CONCERN ABOUT FAT—IT IS LADEN WITH CHOLESTEROL—CAUSES MANY PEOPLE TO COOK WITH OIL INSTEAD. BUT FOR AUTHENTIC FLAVOR, SPLURGE ON THE REAL THING.

SHORTCUT. FIT FOOD PROCESSOR WITH COARSE SHREDDING DISK. FEED POTATOES THROUGH TUBE, ONE AT A TIME. POUR OFF ACCUMULATED LIQUID, THEN EMPTY WORK BOWL INTO A LARGE BOWL. REPEAT UNTIL EACH POTATO IS SHREDDED. WHEN ALL POTATOES ARE SHREDDED, REMOVE SHREDDING DISK AND ATTACH BLADE. CHOP ONION, USING ON-OFF PULSES. PLACE CHOPPED ONION IN BOWL WITH POTATOES. PROCEED AS RECIPE INSTRUCTS.

JELLY doughnuts, called *Sufganiyot*, are an Israeli tradition, most likely modified by European preferences. While the fried dough is considered Middle Eastern, the jelly filling is attributed to European immigrants, probably German. At any rate, these treats fill the Hanukkah bill since they are fried in oil.

JELLY DOUGHNUTS (SUFGANIYOT)

2	ENVELOPES DRY YEAST
4	TABLESPOONS SUGAR (DIVIDED USE)
¾	CUP LUKEWARM MILK
2	EGG YOLKS
1 ½	TABLESPOONS MARGARINE, SOFTENED AT ROOM TEMPERATURE
½	TEASPOON SALT
2 ½	CUPS ALL-PURPOSE FLOUR, SIFTED
1	(20-OUNCE) JAR GRAPE JELLY, APRICOT, OR STRAWBERRY JAM
	OIL FOR DEEP-FRYING
1 ½	CUPS GRANULATED SUGAR OR CONFECTIONERS' SUGAR

Dissolve yeast and 2 tablespoons sugar in warm milk. Stir and let sit until bubbly, about 5 minutes.

In large mixing bowl, combine egg yolks and margarine. Stir in milk and remaining 2 tablespoons sugar, beating well. Sift together salt and flour. Gradually add sifted flour to milk, stirring after each addition, to make a workable dough.

Turn out dough onto a lightly floured board and knead until smooth, about 10 minutes. Lightly rub another large, clean bowl with shortening or margarine. Place dough in bowl, cover and let rise in a warm place, 2 to 2½ hours.

After first rise, turn out dough onto a lightly floured board and knead a couple of times. Let rest about 10 minutes, then roll thin, to about ½-inch thickness. Cut into 2-

inch rounds. Remove scraps. Cover rounds and let rise 15 minutes, or more until doubled in size.

Heat about 2 to 3 inches oil in a deep-sided pan to 375°. Drop doughnuts, a few at a time, turning once, and fry until golden, 2 to 3 minutes on each side. Be careful not to over-cook. The dough will puff when it hits the hot oil. Drain briefly on absorbent paper towels.

Using a tiny spoon, insert a small spoonful of jelly or jam in the top or side of the doughnut. Twirl spoon to release filling and carefully remove spoon through the same hole. Thumbs and fingers are helpful here, too. Roll doughnut in granulated sugar or dust tops with confectioners' sugar. Serve warm.

Makes about 2 dozen.

SUFGANIYOT
(JELLY DOUGHNUTS), P. 54

VIVIENNE CORN, Elaine's mother, shared this Hanukkah recipe, a favorite in their El Paso home.

DOUGHNUT (SUFGANIYOT) DROPS

2	EGGS
¼	CUP SUGAR
1	TEASPOON SALT
2	TABLESPOONS MELTED BUTTER
1 ½	CUPS FLOUR
4	TEASPOONS BAKING POWDER
⅓	CUP MILK
1	(6-OUNCE) PACKAGE CHOCOLATE CHIPS, OPTIONAL
	VEGETABLE OIL FOR FRYING

Place eggs in a large bowl and beat until light yellow and slightly thickened. Add sugar, salt, and butter. Combine flour and baking powder.

Add flour mixture and milk, alternately, to eggs, mixing well after each addition. Stir in chocolate chips, if desired.

Heat 2 to 3 inches of oil in a deep-sided pan over medium-high heat. Oil should be hot, 390° on a candy or deep-fry thermometer.

Drop batter by teaspoons into hot oil and fry until golden, turning as needed to even the color. Remove with slotted spoon and drain on absorbent paper towels. Allow to cool. Sprinkle with confectioners' sugar.

Makes about 2 dozen.

DALLAS baker *extraordinaire* Betty Ablon makes Rugelach, pecan-filled cookies, that are absolutely wonderful. They are also a Hanukkah tradition for some.

RUGELACH

8   OUNCES UNSALTED BUTTER,
        SLIGHTLY SOFTENED

8   OUNCES CREAM CHEESE,
        SLIGHTLY SOFTENED

2   CUPS ALL-PURPOSE FLOUR

½   CUP APRICOT JAM, HEATED TO MELT,
        THEN COOLED (DIVIDED USE)

¼   CUP SUGAR PLUS 2 TEASPOONS
        CINNAMON (DIVIDED USE)

8   OUNCES (1 CUP) FINELY CHOPPED
        PECANS OR PECANS AND RAISINS
        TO MAKE 1 CUP (DIVIDED USE)

In a medium mixing bowl, beat together butter and cream cheese until creamy and light. Beat in flour, ½ cup at a time, to make a soft dough. Shape dough into a ball in the bowl and place bowl in refrigerator. Cover and chill dough for several hours for easier handling.

Preheat oven to 350°.

Divide dough in half. Roll out half the dough on a lightly floured board into a 12-inch circle, ⅛-inch thick, similar to pie crust. Brush lightly with ¼ cup apricot jam. Combine sugar and cinnamon. Sprinkle 1 tablespoon cinnamon-sugar over jam. Spread with half the nuts. Cut circle into 16 wedges. Roll wedges, starting with the long side, and curve each pastry to form a crescent shape. Sprinkle crescents with 1 tablespoon cinnamon-sugar.

Repeat using remaining dough and filling ingredients. Place on an ungreased cookie sheet and bake 18 to 20 minutes.

Makes 32 cookies.

LIGHT sweets like these are excellent for holiday meals with meat on the menu. Both avoid dairy products.

COCONUT MACAROONS

2	LARGE EGG WHITES
⅛	(SCANT) TEASPOON SALT
⅛	TEASPOON CREAM OF TARTAR
½	CUP CONFECTIONERS' SUGAR
1	TEASPOON VANILLA OR ALMOND EXTRACT
1	CUP SWEETENED OR UNSWEETENED SHREDDED DRIED COCONUT

Preheat oven to 250°. Line 2 baking sheets with kitchen parchment paper.

Place egg whites in a medium bowl and allow to come to room temperature. Beat with an electric mixer on high speed until foamy. Add salt and cream of tartar. Continue beating. As whites begin to stiffen, slowly add sugar. Beat until very stiff and glossy.

Using a rubber spatula, gently fold in vanilla or almond flavoring and coconut. Drop by teaspoons on the parchment paper, about ½ inch apart. Batter should not spread.

Bake for 10 minutes. Remove baking sheet and rotate, back to front, in oven. Bake 10 minutes longer, until cookies are very light brown.

For a softer macaroon, slide parchment paper with macaroons onto a damp surface, such as a towels, and let them steam for 1 minute.

Using a spatula, transfer macaroons to racks to cool. Allow macaroons to dry several hours.

Makes 35 to 40 macaroons.

THIS is a great cookie to make when you've had the oven hot for something else. Place meringues in an oven which has been turned off and cooled to about 200°. Leave in oven overnight.

MERINGUE COOKIES

3	EGG WHITES
¼	TEASPOON SALT
¼	TEASPOON CREAM OF TARTAR
½	CUP GRANULATED SUGAR
½	TEASPOON VANILLA
½	CUP FINELY CHOPPED PECANS

Preheat oven to 200°. Line a cookie sheet with kitchen parchment paper.

In a large mixing bowl, beat egg whites with an electric mixer until frothy. Add salt and cream of tartar. Continue beating. As whites begin to stiffen, slowly add the sugar, a tablespoon at a time, until the mixture is stiff and glossy.

Using a rubber spatula, gently fold in vanilla and chopped pecans.

Drop batter by tablespoons onto the parchment paper about 1 inch apart. Bake for 1 hour or until meringues appear dry. Turn off oven and allow to cool in oven overnight.

Remove from cookie sheet and store in an airtight container.

Makes 2 dozen.

THESE Mini-Strudels from Sally Bernstein are excellent for any winter holiday occasion.

MINI-STRUDELS

4	OUNCES CREAM CHEESE, SOFTENED AT ROOM TEMPERATURE
2	STICKS (½ POUND) BUTTER, SOFTENED AT ROOM TEMPERATURE
1	(8-OUNCE) CARTON SOUR CREAM
5–5½	CUPS ALL-PURPOSE FLOUR (SIFT BEFORE MEASURING)
1	(14-OUNCE) JAR STRAWBERRY PRESERVES
1	(14-OUNCE) JAR APRICOT PRESERVES
1	(6-OUNCE) PACKAGE FLAKED COCONUT
2	CUPS RAISINS
1	(8-OUNCE) PACKAGE CHOPPED PECANS
1	CUP (APPROXIMATELY) GRANULATED SUGAR (DIVIDED USE)

In a large bowl, beat together cream cheese, butter, and sour cream. Gradually add flour, mixing by hand, to make a soft, but not sticky, dough. Shape dough into a ball and wrap tightly in plastic. Refrigerate overnight.

Preheat oven to 350°. Grease 2 cookie sheets.

Cut chilled dough into four pieces. Roll out each piece on a floured board until very thin. Spread strawberry preserves on 2 sections and apricot preserves on 2 sections. Sprinkle each section of dough with coconut, raisins, and pecans.

Fold over long sides to seal filling. Fold over ends to form long, narrow rectangle.

Place strudels, seam-side down, on prepared cookie sheets. Sprinkle top of each strudel generously with granulated sugar. Cut through top layer of dough to make 1-inch pieces. Do not separate.

Bake for 45 minutes or until golden. Cool 15 minutes, then cut all the way through to make separate pieces. Separate and allow to cool.

Makes 65 (1-inch) pieces.

ALSO For HANUKKAH

OUR FAMILY USES A MENORAH MY GREAT GRANDMOTHER, RACHEL ROSEN, BROUGHT WITH HER FROM RUSSIA IN 1892. IT IS AN IMPORTANT PART OF OUR FAMILY TRADITION.

Barbara and Larry Glazer

CHRISTMAS

CHICKEN MOLE, P. 65, WITH RICE, P. 131;
FLAN, P. 118, GARNISHED WITH
STRAWBERRIES; SWEET TAMALES, P. 115

*N*othing beats a Texas Christmas. No other holiday is so eagerly anticipated, so fervently prepared for and so filled with memories.

A Texas Christmas reflects the richest blend of cultural influences of all the holidays, incorporating customs and traditions practiced by the many people who have come to call themselves Texans.

Twinkle lights in the pine trees of East Texas, *luminaria* in San Antonio, the capitol in Austin decked out for the holidays, elaborate theme decorations in department stores in Dallas and Houston, cowboy manger scenes in West Texas—all these are images of a Texas Christmas.

No traditions are more beautiful and symbolic than Hispanic folk expressions: *luminaria* (candle-lit lanterns), *ristra* (dried red chili) wreaths, piñatas, and sparkling lights. Of course, German and English practices permeate Christmas celebrations as well, particularly in some of the signature foods: fruitcake, coconut cake, and egg nog.

While the scenes may differ with location, customs, and geography, many of the same holiday foods can be found in all locales throughout the state.

It is a holiday of mix-and-match traditions. Enchiladas and mince pie may show up on the same buffet.

CHRISTMAS FEASTING

While the menu for Thanksgiving is virtually set in stone, Christmas feasts can be formal or casual. The main gathering may be on Christmas Eve as a nighttime meal. It may take place Christmas Day in the late morning as brunch, around the noon hour or early afternoon as dinner, or as an all-day open house.

And, often, families change their rituals from year to year, depending on a wide variety of circumstances, not the least of which is weather.

As a native Texan, I can remember playing outdoors in shorts after opening presents on some Christmases, and, during other holiday seasons, waiting for frozen pipes to thaw so I could rinse the vegetables. Yes, Texas weather varies considerably during the winter. So do our tastes.

CHRISTMAS EVE

Christmas Eve is a time when many Texans harken to their roots, varied though they may be. For some, it is a time to take special care to remember one's heritage through a particular dish or dishes. That might be sauerkraut and venison sausage, barbecue, or lasagna.

No Christmas Eve tradition is any richer than that of the Hispanic table. Mole is the dark, rich chocolate and ground chile-based sauce so characteristic of Mexican holiday cuisine.

The following recipe is based on Dallas photographer Juan Garcia's mouth-watering description and adaptations of several recipes. Author Linda West Eckhardt *(The Only Texas Cookbook)* devised the shortcut addition of peanut butter to bottled mole sauce to better approximate the traditional sauce using dried, ground chilies, and toasted nuts and seeds.

In Mexico, this traditional dish uses turkey pieces.

CHICKEN MOLE

8	PIECES CHICKEN (WHOLE CHICKEN CUT-UP, OR ANY COMBINATION OF DESIRED SERVING-SIZE PIECES SUCH AS LEGS, THIGHS, AND BREASTS HALVES)
1½	TEASPOONS SALT, OR TO TASTE (DIVIDED USE)
1	TEASPOON PEPPER, OR TO TASTE
1	(8¼-OUNCE) JAR MOLE SAUCE
½	CUP ENCHILADA SAUCE OR TOMATO SAUCE
½–1	CUP CHICKEN STOCK
1	TABLESPOON SMOOTH PEANUT BUTTER
1	SQUARE DARK, UNSWEETENED CHOCOLATE
1	TABLESPOON SUGAR

Preheat oven to 350°. Heat a deep, ovenproof skillet or Dutch oven over medium heat. Add chicken pieces, and cook until brown on all sides, about 20 minutes. Season chicken

with 1 teaspoon salt and pepper. Cover pan with lid and place in oven 20 to 30 minutes, until chicken juices run clear.

Meanwhile, in a large saucepan, combine mole sauce, enchilada or tomato sauce, and chicken broth, beginning with ½ cup. Add more as needed to adjust consistency and flavor. Heat to boiling; reduce heat to simmer. Stir in peanut butter, chocolate and sugar. Cook and stir until chocolate is melted, about 5 minutes. Continue simmering 10 minutes longer. Season with ½ teaspoon salt, or to taste. If sauce seems too thick, add just enough water or chicken stock to thin to desired consistency.

Remove chicken from oven and pour sauce over chicken. Reduce oven to 300°. Return chicken to oven, covered, and bake for 30 to 40 minutes or until chicken is tender, almost falling off the bone.

Serve with white or Mexican rice (p.67) or tortillas. This recipe doubles easily.

Makes 4 servings.

WE ALWAYS HAD TAMALES ON CHRISTMAS AND NEW YEAR'S AND SOMETIMES MOLE, BEFORE OR AFTER MIDNIGHT MASS. I CAN TASTE THAT DARK, RED SAUCE RIGHT NOW AND FEEL THE CHICKEN IN MY FINGERS, THE MEAT SO TENDER IT SLIPPED OFF THE BONES. IT WAS SERVED WITH RICE, BUT YOU PICKED UP THE CHICKEN WITH YOUR FINGERS TO EAT IT. THE BROWNER THE SAUCE, THE SWEETER IT WAS. THE REDDER IT WAS, THE HOTTER.

Juan Garcia

THIS is the kind of red-orange rice you get in Mexican restaurants. It is a meal in itself with refried beans and tortillas. It is also a must with enchiladas.

MEXICAN RICE

1	(16-OUNCE) CAN WHOLE TOMATOES, INCLUDING LIQUID
1	TABLESPOON VEGETABLE OIL OR BACON DRIPPINGS
1	CUP LONG-GRAIN RICE
1	CUP CHOPPED ONION
½	CUP FINELY CHOPPED CARROTS
2	CLOVES GARLIC, FINELY CHOPPED
1	(4-OUNCE) CAN CHOPPED GREEN CHILIES, DRAINED, OR 3 TABLESPOONS FINELY CHOPPED GREEN BELL PEPPER
¼	TEASPOON CUMIN POWDER
1	(14½-OUNCE) CAN CHICKEN OR BEEF STOCK
1	TEASPOON SALT, OR TO TASTE
½	TEASPOON PEPPER, OR TO TASTE

Empty tomatoes and their liquid into a 1-pint measuring cup. Use the back of a wooden spoon or edge of a knife to break tomatoes into bite-size pieces. Set aside.

Heat oil in a large skillet over medium heat. Add rice, stirring frequently, and cook until rice begins to brown. Add onion and carrots and cook until onions begin to soften. Lower heat, if necessary, to prevent rice from getting too dark. Stir in garlic.

Add tomatoes and their liquid, green chilies (or peppers), chicken or beef stock, cumin, salt, and pepper. Bring liquid to a boil. Reduce heat, cover, and simmer until rice is tender and liquid is absorbed, about 20 to 25 minutes.

This recipe doubles easily.

Makes 4 servings.

Janis and Joe Pinnelli make a mean pan of lasagna at their Austin home on Christmas Eve. Joe, the true Texas *paisano*, makes the sauce. Janis puts the whole thing together.

Joe developed the sauce recipe by watching his grandmother cooking in Italy and by trial-and-error in his own kitchen. Use it anytime a basic marinara sauce is called for.

Christmas Eve Lasagna

The Sauce

4	(28-OUNCE) CANS WHOLE TOMATOES
1	(6-OUNCE) CAN TOMATO PASTE
2	TABLESPOONS DRIED CRUSHED OREGANO (NOT POWDERED)
1	TABLESPOON DRIED THYME
1	TABLESPOON DRIED ROSEMARY
1	TEASPOON SALT, OR TO TASTE
¼	CUP VIRGIN OLIVE OIL
4	GARLIC CLOVES, CRUSHED
2	TABLESPOONS SUGAR

The Filling

3	CUPS FRESH RICOTTA CHEESE
2	EGGS, LIGHTLY BEATEN
½	CUP GRATED ROMANO CHEESE
2	TABLESPOONS PARSLEY FLAKES
1	TEASPOON SALT, OR TO TASTE
½	TEASPOON PEPPER, OR TO TASTE
1	POUND LASAGNA NOODLES, COOKED ACCORDING TO PACKAGE DIRECTIONS
1	(16-OUNCE) POUND MOZZARELLA CHEESE, SLICED
	GRATED PARMESAN CHEESE, FOR PASSING AT TABLE

To Make Sauce

Since sauce scorches easily, use a large heavy-bottomed saucepan, stock pot, or Dutch oven, preferably with a non-stick surface.

Place canned tomatoes and their liquid into the pan. Use a small paring knife to remove any tomato cores. Add tomato paste.

Use hands (or back of a large wooden spoon) to crush the tomatoes and combine with the tomato paste. Tomatoes should be in small pieces. The mixture should be soupy and lumpy.

Combine oregano, thyme, rosemary, and salt into a blender. Blend to a smooth powder.

Add powdered spices, garlic, and olive oil to tomatoes, stirring well. Place pot on stove over low heat. Bring liquid to a simmer and simmer for 1 hour and 30 minutes. Stir almost continually during cooking since sauce scorches easily. Use a spatula to scrape sauce from bottom to avoid sticking.

Add sugar 15 minutes before the end of cooking. Do not add sugar too soon, or sauce will stick. Overcooking will result in a bitter taste. For optimum flavor, make the sauce a day ahead and refrigerate overnight.

Use over spaghetti or any other recipe that calls for a rich marinara sauce. The sauce freezes well. Reheat and simmer to desired consistency.

To Assemble Lasagna

Allow sauce to cool. Meanwhile, stir together in a large bowl, the ricotta cheese, eggs, parsley, Romano cheese, salt, and pepper.

Preheat oven to 350°. Line bottom of large, flat baking dish or roasting pan (at least 9 x 13-inches) with half the cooked noodles. Cover with half the cheese mixture, half the sliced mozzarella and a generous layer of sauce, thick enough to seal the edges. Repeat with remaining noodles, cheese mixture, and sliced mozzarella. Cover with a generous layer of sauce. Reserve and heat some sauce for passing at table.

Bake lasagna, uncovered, for 30 to 45 minutes or until heated through. Cut into squares and serve. Serve with additional sauce and Parmesan cheese, passed at the table.

OTHER IDEAS *For* CHRISTMAS EVE

Variation

Double ingredients for filling and make 2 pans of lasagna. Add 1 pound of crumbled, cooked and drained Italian sausage or ground beef to sauce along with spices. Cook as above.

Makes 8 to 10 servings.

CHRISTMAS BREAKFAST

Christmas breakfast can be as simple as bakery pastries or as elaborate as Fried Quail with Cheese Grits and Fruit Salad. It is a wonderful meal at which to blend the best of several traditions, Country Gravy with Sausage and Fluffy Biscuits, Tex-Mex Eggs, Southern-Fried Quail, and various pastries including Czech Kolaches.

FRIED QUAIL, P. 71, WITH
CREAM GRAVY, P.72;
SLICED FRESH TOMATOES;
CHEESE GRITS, P.75

WHETHER you buy them or bag them, quail are a wonderful delicacy. The tender birds are flavorful and adapt well to many methods of cooking. Pen-raised quail, available in supermarkets and by mail order, are larger than the wild birds. If you're lucky enough to have wild quail, make a few extra.

FRIED QUAIL

8	QUAIL
1	CUP BUTTERMILK
1	CUP UNBLEACHED FLOUR
2	TEASPOONS SALT, OR TO TASTE
1	TEASPOON PEPPER, OR TO TASTE
	OIL FOR FRYING

Rinse quail and pat dry. Split backs of quail so birds can open flat, breast up with legs and wings flattened.

Place quail in resealable plastic bag. Pour buttermilk over and allow to marinate 30 minutes to several hours, or overnight. Remove quail from buttermilk and allow to drain.

Combine flour, salt, and pepper in large plastic bag, shaking to mix well. Drop quail into flour mixture, one at a time, shaking well to coat evenly. Remove from bag and place on a layer of wax paper. Repeat with remaining quail. Allow quail to sit for 10 to 20 minutes to "set" the batter.

Heat 1-inch vegetable or corn oil in a heavy skillet, preferably cast iron. Oil should be hot, about 375°.

Gently, slide a quail into hot oil, breast side down. Allow oil to recover temperature so that the quail floats before adding next bird. Fry 2 to 3 birds at a time. Each quail should have room to float in the pan without touching. Cook until golden and crisp on breast side, about 5 minutes. Turn and fry on back side until golden brown and crisp, about 3 to 4 minutes.

Because quail is white meat, it cooks rather quickly, like chicken breast.

Remove quail from skillet and drain briefly on paper towels. Keep warm. Serve with Cream Gravy or Texas Wine Sauce (p. 81).

Smothered Quail

Preheat oven to 325°. Arrange fried quail in a 9 x 13-inch baking dish. Pour in about ⅛-inch water, Cream Gravy or Texas Wine Sauce. Cover with foil and bake for 30 to 45 minutes. Serve with additional gravy or sauce.

This is the mother's milk of Texas cooking. It can be found on plates from breakfast through dinner.

Cream Gravy

3	TABLESPOONS VEGETABLE OIL, MELTED BUTTER, OR DRIPPINGS FROM FRYING
¼	CUP FLOUR
1	CUP (EACH) WARM MILK AND WARM WATER, MORE LIQUID IF NEEDED
1	TEASPOON SALT, OR TO TASTE
1	TEASPOON PEPPER, OR TO TASTE

Heat butter, oil, or drippings in large skillet over medium heat. (If making gravy after cooking sausage, frying quail or other meat, by all means pour all but three tablespoons of drippings. Keep the browned bits in the bottom of the skillet, too.)

Stir in flour and cook until bubbly, scraping up any bits that may stick to bottom of pan. Add milk and water, stirring constantly with wire whisk or the back of a slotted spoon. Lower heat and simmer until thickened. Add salt and pepper to taste. Serve over Fried Quail, mashed potatoes, or just about any meat or fowl, particularly if it is fried.

SAUSAGE GRAVY

Crumble ¼ to ½ pound bulk sausage into skillet over medium heat. Cook until brown. Drain sausage on paper toweling. Reserve 3 tablespoons of pan drippings. Discard remainder. Make gravy as above, using pan drippings. Add cooked sausage when gravy thickens. Season to taste. Serve over biscuits or scrambled eggs.

Makes 8 servings.

THIS is a basic biscuit recipe. Handle the dough as little as possible. But making the extra "turn" on the dough gives lighter, fluffier biscuits. The principle is the same as puff pastry.

BISCUITS

2	CUPS SIFTED FLOUR (SIFT BEFORE MEASURING)
3	TEASPOONS BAKING POWDER
1	TEASPOON SALT
⅓	CUP SHORTENING
¾	CUP COLD MILK

Preheat oven to 450°.

Sift together flour, baking powder, and salt. Cut in shortening using two knives, a pastry cutter, or fingers. Mixture should resemble coarse cornmeal. Make a well in dry ingredients. Add milk and mix just until soft dough forms.

Turn dough out onto lightly floured board. Knead lightly 2 or 3 times and pat with fingers or roll out dough about ½-inch thick. Fold over dough in thirds and re-roll into a ½-inch thick oblong, handling as little as possible.

Cut with a 2-inch biscuit cutter or flour the rim of a water glass and use as a cutter. Place biscuits on ungreased baking sheet and bake 10 to 12 minutes until golden brown.

Makes 10 to 12 biscuits.

THIS is a traditional Tex-Mex recipe for scrambled eggs.

MIGAS

3	CORN TORTILLAS
1	TABLESPOON VEGETABLE OIL
½	CUP ONION, CHOPPED FINE
6	EGGS
6	TABLESPOONS WATER
½	TEASPOON SALT, OR TO TASTE
¼	TEASPOON PEPPER, OR TO TASTE
1	CUP CHOPPED TOMATO, OPTIONAL
½	CUP CHOPPED GREEN CHILIES, OPTIONAL
½	CUP GRATED CHEDDAR CHEESE

SHORTCUT. COARSELY CRUSH ABOUT 2 CUPS PACKAGED TORTILLA CHIPS AND SUBSTITUTE FOR CORN TORTILLAS. OMIT CRISPING IN OIL AND ADD DIRECTLY TO EGGS.

Cut tortillas into bite-size pieces, about the size of small corn chips. Heat oil in large skillet over medium heat. Add tortillas pieces, stirring to distribute evenly and cook until crisp, 2 to 3 minutes. Drain on paper toweling and reserve.

Add onion to skillet and cook until soft and golden around the edges. Combine eggs and water, 2 tablespoons at a time, beating until frothy. Add salt and pepper to taste. Pour eggs into skillet. Add tortilla chips. Stir to evenly cook eggs.

When eggs are almost firm, add tomatoes and chilies, if desired, and cheese; stir. Cook just until cheese melts and eggs are set.

Serve immediately.

Makes 6 to 8 servings.

CHEDDAR CHEESE GRITS

4	CUPS MILK
4	TABLESPOONS BUTTER (DIVIDED USE)
1	CUP GRITS, QUICK-COOKING OR OLD-FASHIONED (NOT INSTANT)
1	CUP SHREDDED CHEDDAR CHEESE
1	TEASPOON SALT, OR TO TASTE
½	TEASPOON WHITE PEPPER, OR TO TASTE
2–3	DROPS RED PEPPER SAUCE, OR TO TASTE

Combine milk, 2 tablespoons butter, and grits over medium heat in a large saucepan. When milk begins to boil, lower heat. Simmer and stir over low heat, according to package directions, about 3 to 5 minutes for quick-cooking grits, 10 to 12 minutes for old-fashioned, or until thickened.

Remove from heat. Stir in 2 tablespoons butter, cheese, salt, pepper and red pepper sauce, to taste. Adjust texture with additional milk, if needed. May be made ahead, stored in refrigerator, and reheated on top of stove over low heat.

Makes 8 servings.

THE town of West, Texas, just north of Waco on I-35 about halfway between Dallas and Austin, is kolache territory. This Czech community celebrates its heritage annually with a Labor Day festival. The rest of us can celebrate with a stop at one of the several bakeries in town on the main drag, just a quick detour off the highway.

Can't make it to West? Try these.

KOLACHES
(CZECH SWEET ROLLS)

2	(PACKAGES) DRY YEAST
½	CUP LUKEWARM (105°–115°) WATER
1½	CUPS WARM MILK
½	CUP BUTTER
½	CUP SUGAR
1	TEASPOON SALT
1	EGG, BEATEN
5–6	CUPS FLOUR
	FILLINGS (SEE BELOW)

Sprinkle yeast over warm water, stirring to activate. Set aside.

Heat milk to almost boiling. Remove from heat. Add butter and stir to melt. Add sugar and salt. Pour into large mixing bowl and allow to cool to lukewarm. Stir in egg and add yeast mixture.

Add flour gradually, about 2 cups at a time, stirring after each addition to make a soft, sticky dough. Do not add too much flour or kolaches will be dense and dry. Cover and let rise until doubled in size, about 1 hour. Begin preparing fillings while dough rises.

Grease a baking sheet well. Rub hands with grease, too. Using well-greased hands, shape dough into 2-inch balls. Place on prepared baking sheet about 2 inches apart. Cover with damp cloth and let rise again until doubled in size, about 30 to 45 minutes.

Preheat oven to 350°. Using your thumb, make an indention in the center of each roll, leaving a 1-inch rim. Allow to rest 10 minutes. Fill with about 1 tablespoon fruit or cheese filling and bake for 20 to 25 minutes or until golden.

Makes about 3 dozen.

Fillings

• Combine 1 cup dried fruit (6-ounce package of apricots, prunes, or apples) in just enough water to cover in a small saucepan. Bring water to a boil, reduce heat, and simmer until fruit is soft, about 10 to 12 minutes. Drain fruit and chop fine. Return to saucepan along with 1 cup sugar, 1½ teaspoons lemon juice, and 4 tablespoons butter. Cook and stir over low heat until mixture thickens like jam, about 10 minutes. Cool completely.

• Combine 1 cup cream cheese or dry curd cottage cheese with ½ cup sugar, 1 egg yolk, 1 teaspoon vanilla, ⅛ teaspoon salt, and 3 tablespoons melted butter. Mix until smooth.

CHRISTMAS DINNER

The big sit-down isn't reserved for Thanksgiving alone. But there's much more latitude with the Christmas menu. Often, a Christmas table will hold a variety of meats: perhaps ham and turkey, maybe venison or a beef roast.

Christmas is a time when the focus is scattered: religious celebrations, gifts, decorations, parties. Food is important, but just a part of the mix. That gives a Texas cook lots of room for family favorites.

And it doesn't matter when you sit down to a Christmas dinner. It can be on Christmas day, Christmas Eve, or anytime during the holiday when family and friends can be together.

BEEF is as almost as traditional for Christmas as turkey is for Thanksgiving. In a state where much of the lore and culture are based on ranching, that is understandable. But the hunting tradition is important here also. So you'll find plenty of wild game recipes on holiday tables.

AS WITH THANKSGIVING, GETTING A HEAD START ON CHRISTMAS DINNER IS THE KEY TO SUCCESS IN TIMING. THIS IS EVEN MORE DIFFICULT TO ACHIEVE AT CHRISTMAS BECAUSE THERE IS SO MUCH MORE GOING ON. THE GOOD NEWS? THE MEAL CAN BE SIMPLER, AT LEAST IN TERMS OF THE NUMBER OF DISHES REQUIRED TO FULFILL EXPECTATIONS OF TRADITION.

Roast Standing Rib *of* Beef

1	(5–8-POUND) STANDING RIB ROAST
3–4	CLOVES GARLIC, CUT INTO SLIVERS, OPTIONAL
2	TEASPOONS SALT, OR TO TASTE
1	TEASPOON PEPPER, OR TO TASTE

Remove roast from refrigerator 1 hour before roasting to allow meat to come to room temperature. Preheat oven to 325°.

If desired, pierce surface of roast at intervals with the tip of a sharp knife or ice pick and insert a sliver of garlic.

Place roast, fat side up, in open roasting pan. Place it on a rack, or let the ribs serve as a natural rack to keep the meat from sitting in the fat as it drips into the pan.

Do not add liquid to the pan; do not cover. Place meat in oven and roast for 18 to 20 minutes per pound, or until meat thermometer reads 140° for rare and up to 170° for well-done.

Medium-rare, about 145°, is optimum for flavor and tenderness. A roast that registers 140° to 145° when the meat thermometer is inserted in the thickest part, not touching fat or bone, will ensure that there are nice rare slices in the middle. Naturally, slices from the exterior will tend to be more done, thus ensuring a degree of doneness to make everyone happy.

Slice ½-inch thick.

Makes 10 to 12 servings.

Variation

For Beef Tenderloin, ask butcher to fold over and tie ends of 5-pound beef tenderloin to create a roast of uniform thickness. (Plan on 3 servings per pound for this boneless cut.) Insert slivers of fresh garlic, if desired. Rub lightly with butter or vegetable oil. Preheat oven to 400°. Place on a rack in a shallow roasting pan. Follow instructions for 500° Method.

ALLOW 2 TO 3 SERVINGS PER POUND WHEN BUYING A STANDING RIB ROAST. ASK THE BUTCHER TO SEPARATE THE ROAST FROM THE BONES, AND THEN TO TIE IT BACK IN POSITION. THIS ALLOWS FOR EASIER SLICING WHILE RETAINING THE NATURAL ROASTING RACK FORMED BY THE RIBS. REMOVE STRING BEFORE SLICING.

The 500° Method for Perfect Roast Beef

This works for beef roasts such as standing rib or tenderloins that are best served medium rare. It is not a satisfactory method for preparing pot roasts or other less tender cuts that are more tender with long, slow cooking. Remove any size beef roast from refrigerator 1 hour before roasting. Preheat oven to 500°. Season roast as desired. Place roast in open roasting pan with shallow sides and cook for exactly 5 minutes per pound. Example: an 8-pound roast should cook for 40 minutes at 500°. Immediately, turn off oven. Do not open the oven door. Leave roast in hot oven for exactly 2 hours. Remove roast from oven. It will be cooked medium-rare. Caution: This method produces a lot of spatter in the oven if you're cooking a roast such as a standing rib with a thick layer of fat. Don't be surprised at some smoke, and expect to clean the oven.

IN recent years, the popularity of spiral-cut hams with a honey crust have put a serious dent in the home preparation of ham. For good reason. The product is excellent and convenient. But for a classic, home-baked ham, try this recipe.

BROWN SUGAR-BAKED HAM

1	(8–10-POUND) FULLY COOKED HAM, BONE-IN
2–3	TABLESPOONS GROUND CINNAMON
2	TABLESPOONS GROUND CLOVES
	WHOLE CLOVES, OPTIONAL
½	CUP BROWN SUGAR, PACKED
1	TABLESPOON YELLOW OR DIJON MUSTARD
1	TABLESPOON FLOUR

Preheat oven to 300°–325°. If using a cured ham with skin on, cut away skin from ham, but leave the fat. Rub ham with cinnamon and cloves to cover completely. Wrap tightly in foil and bake for 15 minutes per pound. Cool ham slightly and scrape away cinnamon and cloves; discard.

SHORTCUT. PURCHASE A 5-POUND FULLY-COOKED BONELESS HAM WITH SKIN AND FAT ALREADY TRIMMED. PLACE HAM IN DOUBLE LAYER OF FOIL (LARGE ENOUGH TO WRAP HAM COMPLETELY) IN BOTTOM OF A SHALLOW ROASTING PAN. POUR OVER HAM 1 CUP APPLE JUICE, CRANBERRY JUICE, GINGER ALE, OR BEER. WRAP HAM TIGHTLY. PLACE IN OVEN AND BAKE FOR 15 MINUTES PER POUND. REMOVE FROM OVEN AND SMEAR TOP WITH MUSTARD AND BROWN SUGAR/FLOUR MIXTURE; OMIT OPTIONAL WHOLE CLOVES. RETURN TO OVEN, UNCOVERED, FOR 30 TO 35 MINUTES TO MELT AND CARAMELIZE THE SUGAR. COOL SLIGHTLY BEFORE SLICING AND SERVING.

Coat ham with thin smear of mustard. If desired, cut diamond pattern into fat layer and place a whole clove in each diamond as a garnish. Combine brown sugar with flour. Pat brown sugar over ham to evenly cover fat layer. Use additional brown sugar, if needed, to thoroughly coat ham. Return ham, uncovered, to oven for 30 to 35 minutes to melt and caramelize the sugar. Cool before slicing and serving.

Makes 10 to 12 servings.

THE choicest cut of venison is the backstrap, which resembles a beef tenderloin in appearance (although smaller) and tenderness. Treat as you would a tenderloin; roast it or grill it no more than medium-rare, although rare with a warm center is preferable because the cut is so naturally lean.

ROAST VENISON BACKSTRAP

2	(1½ TO 2-POUND) VENISON BACKSTRAPS
1–2	TEASPOONS EACH SALT AND PEPPER, OR TO TASTE; OR SUBSTITUTE 1 TO 2 TEASPOONS FAVORITE STEAK SEASONING BLEND, TO TASTE
1	TABLESPOON VEGETABLE OIL
2	TABLESPOONS BUTTER

If backstraps are more than 2-inches thick, preheat oven to 400°.

Heat a heavy skillet with ovenproof handle over medium-high heat. Lightly coat with non-stick cooking spray. Add backstraps and cook on all sides until brown. Internal temperature should not cook past medium rare (140° on a meat thermometer). Thick backstraps may require 3 to 5 minutes in the oven to cook to desired degree of doneness.

Remove from heat and allow juices to settle, about 10 minutes. Wrap backstrap in foil to keep warm.

Over medium heat, whisk butter into pan juices, 1 tablespoon at a time, just until melted. Adjust seasoning as desired.

Place backstrap on serving platter and slice into ½- to 1-inch thick medallions. Drizzle with pan juices.

Makes 6 to 8 servings.

Variation

To grill backstraps, light coals and cook until gray ash covers the surface. Oil and season backstrap as above. Place on hot grill and cook as you would a steak, until medium rare, turning once to cook all sides. Remove from grill and spread butter over top of each backstrap. Slice and serve with accumulated juices.

Makes 6 to 8 servings.

THIS particular sauce will work well for beef or wild game, including game birds.

But it is particularly nice with roast prime rib of beef or roast venison backstrap.

TEXAS WINE SAUCE

2	CUPS BEEF STOCK
1	CUP TEXAS CABERNET SAUVIGNON, MERLOT, OR OTHER DRY RED WINE
2	TABLESPOONS BUTTER
1½	TABLESPOONS CORNSTARCH
2	TABLESPOONS WATER
1	TEASPOON EACH SALT AND PEPPER, OR TO TASTE, OR SUBSTITUTE YOUR FAVORITE SEASONING BLEND

In a medium saucepan, combine stock and wine. Place over high heat and bring liquid to a boil. Reduce heat and cook until liquid is reduced by half to make about 1½ cups sauce.

Whisk in butter. Combine cornstarch and water to make a smooth paste. Whisk into sauce and cook over low heat, just until thickened. Add salt and pepper or seasoning blend to taste. Keep warm in a thermos bottle or double boiler until ready to serve. Reheat gently; do not allow to boil.

Makes 1½ cups, about 6 servings.

TIP. ADD PAN JUICES FROM COOKING TO SAUCE FOR ADDITIONAL FLAVOR AND RICHNESS. IF PAN JUICES ARE DEFATTED, ADD ALL THE JUICES TO THE SAUCE AND THICKEN TO DESIRED CONSISTENCY. IF ADDING PAN DRIPPINGS (MOSTLY FAT), ADD 2 TABLESPOONS AND OMIT BUTTER.

SHORTCUT. USE A PACKAGED GRAVY SUCH AS THE KNORR HUNTER MUSHROOM AND GRAVY MIX OR KNORR CLASSIC SAUCE PEPPERCORN SAUCE MIX. SUBSTITUTE WINE FOR ¼ OF THE LIQUID CALLED FOR AND COOK ACCORDING TO PACKAGE INSTRUCTIONS. JUST BEFORE SERVING, STIR IN 1 TABLESPOON DRY SHERRY OR BRANDY.

SOME holidays just aren't complete without a congealed salad to add color and a touch of sweet. Here is a sixties' classic that also goes well with roasted or grilled meats.

CHERRY COLA SALAD

1	(16½-OUNCE) CAN DARK CHERRIES
1	(8-OUNCE) CAN CRUSHED PINEAPPLE
1	CUP CHOPPED PECANS
1	(12-OUNCE) CAN COLA (NOT DIET)
2	PACKAGES BLACK CHERRY GELATIN
	LETTUCE LEAVES AND MAYONNAISE FOR GARNISH, OPTIONAL

Lightly coat a 1½-quart gelatin mold or 9 x 9-inch casserole with nonstick cooking spray. Set aside.

Drain juice from cherries and pineapple; reserve juice in 2-cup measure. Add just enough water to make 2 cups. Heat juice and water to boiling. Combine with gelatin in a medium mixing bowl. Stir until gelatin dissolves, about 2 to 3 minutes. Pour cola into gelatin.

Place gelatin mixture in refrigerator and chill until gelatin begins to set. The mixture should be thick and somewhat jiggly, but not firm. Fold in drained pineapple, cherries, and pecans. Mixture should be thick enough to suspend ingredients evenly throughout gelatin.

Transfer to prepared mold or dish. Refrigerate until firm.

Unmold by dipping bottom of mold into hot water and inverting onto a serving dish. Loosen sides with edge of knife, if needed, or cut gelatin into 16 (2¼-inch) squares and serve on lettuce leaves. Garnish each square with a small dollop of mayonnaise, if desired.

Makes 10 to 12 servings, with leftovers.

A CHRISTMAS table may, or may not, include turkey and dressing. But there's always room for some potatoes. Baked Mashed Potatoes (see p. 84) are a classic, but consider these spud options as well.

POTATOES AU GRATIN

5	LARGE (ABOUT 2½ TO 3 POUNDS) RUSSET POTATOES
1½	CUPS SHREDDED CHEDDAR CHEESE
6	TABLESPOONS BUTTER (DIVIDED USE)
1	CUP SOUR CREAM
1	TEASPOON SALT, OR TO TASTE
½	TEASPOON PEPPER, OR TO TASTE
3	GREEN ONIONS, CHOPPED, INCLUDING GREEN PARTS, OPTIONAL
½	CUP CRUSHED POTATO CHIPS OR CRACKER CRUMBS, OPTIONAL

Preheat oven to 325° to 350°. Coat a 2-quart casserole dish with non-stick spray.

Place whole, unpeeled potatoes in large saucepan with enough cold water to cover. Cook over high heat until water boils. Reduce heat so that water continues at a slow boil and cook potatoes until easily pierced with a fork, about 30 minutes.

Allow to cool slightly. Peel off skins and cut potatoes into quarters. Place in large mixing bowl. Using a potato masher or fork, coarsely mash potatoes so the texture is crumbly, almost a chopped consistency. Set aside.

Combine cheese and 4 tablespoons butter in large saucepan over low heat. Sir until cheese is almost melted. Remove from heat and stir in sour cream. Fold cheese mixture into potatoes along with salt, pepper, and onions.

Melt 2 tablespoons butter. Sprinkle crushed potato chips or cracker crumbs over top of potatoes, if desired. Drizzle melted butter over top of casserole.

Makes 10 to 12 servings.

TWICE-BAKED POTATOES

5	LARGE (2½ TO 3 POUNDS) RUSSET POTATOES, UNPEELED
1	(3-OUNCE) PACKAGE CREAM CHEESE, SOFTENED AT ROOM TEMPERATURE
½	CUP SOUR CREAM
¾–1¼	CUPS WARM MILK OR HALF-AND-HALF
6	TABLESPOONS BUTTER (DIVIDED USE)
1	TEASPOON SALT, OR TO TASTE
½	TEASPOON WHITE PEPPER, OR TO TASTE
6	TABLESPOONS GRATED PARMESAN CHEESE, OPTIONAL

Preheat oven to 425°. Rinse potatoes and dry. Pierce each potato several times with a fork. Rub each potato lightly with butter. Place potatoes directly on middle rack of oven and bake until tender, about 1 hour to 1 hour and 15 minutes. The potatoes should yield when squeezed lightly wearing an oven mitt.

Remove potatoes from oven. Wearing a mitt in one hand, slice potatoes in half lengthwise. Scoop out hot potato pulp into a large mixing bowl; reserve potato shells. Be careful not to tear shells.

Using electric beaters, beat baked potato pulp on low speed, adding cream cheese, sour cream, milk, 4 tablespoons butter, salt, and pepper. When potatoes begin to get smooth, increase speed to high and continue beating until quite smooth. Adjust consistency and flavor with milk, cream cheese, butter, and sour cream, as needed. The texture should be smooth and spoonable, but not runny. Season to taste with salt and pepper.

Spoon potato mixture back into shells, creating small peaks. Sprinkle each potato with Parmesan cheese. Melt remaining 2 tablespoons butter and drizzle over potatoes. Lower oven temperature to 325° to 350°. Return potatoes to oven and bake until cheese melts and edges are golden, about 20 minutes.

If desired, stuffed potato shells may be made ahead and refrigerated until just before serving time. Finish baking, allowing 30 to 35 minutes for reheating and browning.

Makes 10 to 12 servings.

THE Rio Grande Valley is a garden of eatin' (excuse the pun, I just couldn't resist) with the variety of fruits and vegetables grown in this semitropical climate. Red grapefruit are the best-known of the winter crops but other vegetables, such as spinach, abound. There are, of course, some vegetable dishes that lend themselves to winter feasting regardless of season, such as green beans and corn.

Dress up Texas vegetables for the holiday according to Lone Star standards.

FRESH SPINACH SALAD *with* TEXAS GRAPEFRUIT

2	(10-OUNCE) PACKAGES FRESH SPINACH, OR 4 BUNCHES LEAF SPINACH
2	RUBY RED OR RIO RED GRAPEFRUIT, PEELED, OR 1 (11-OUNCE) CAN MANDARIN ORANGE SECTIONS, DRAINED
½	CUP CHOPPED, TOASTED PECANS
½	CUP LIGHT OLIVE OIL
¼	CUP RASPBERRY VINAIGRETTE
½	TEASPOON SALT, OR TO TASTE
¼	TEASPOON PEPPER, OR TO TASTE
½	TEASPOON MAPLE SYRUP
⅛	TEASPOON MINCED SERRANO CHILE, OPTIONAL

SHORTCUTS

• INSTEAD OF REMOVING MEMBRANE AND SEPARATING GRAPEFRUIT INTO SECTIONS, CUT PEELED GRAPEFRUIT INTO THIN ROUNDS, LIKE WAGON WHEELS. SLICE WHEELS INTO HALF CIRCLES.

• SUBSTITUTE ½ TO ¾ CUP BOTTLED CATALINA SALAD DRESSING FOR HOMEMADE RASPBERRY VINAIGRETTE.

Tear spinach leaves from stems. Place spinach leaves in sink full of cold water. Place in colander to drain. Transfer to several layers of dish towels to dry completely. If using bunch spinach, rinse two or three times in sink full of water to remove any sand.

SPINACH SALAD, P. 85

Dry spinach leaves between layers of dish towels. Place spinach leaves in large salad bowl, tearing large leaves into bite-size pieces. Separate grapefruit into sections and cut sections into bite-size pieces. Toss with spinach.

To Make Vinaigrette

Combine oil, vinegar, salt, pepper, maple syrup, and minced serrano, if desired, in a jar with tight-fitting lid or whisk together until salt is dissolved. Pour over salad and toss to evenly coat ingredients. Garnish with chopped pecans.

Makes 8 to 10 servings.

CORN CASSEROLE

2	(10-OUNCE) PACKAGES FROZEN WHOLE KERNEL CORN, THAWED AND DRAINED
1	(8¾-OUNCE) CAN CREAMED CORN
2	EGGS, WELL-BEATEN
½	CUP MILK OR HALF-AND-HALF
1	TEASPOON SALT, OR TO TASTE
½	TEASPOON PEPPER, OR TO TASTE
¼	CUP GRATED MONTEREY JACK CHEESE WITH JALAPEÑOS
½	CUP CRUSHED CRACKER CRUMBS, OPTIONAL
1	TABLESPOON BUTTER, MELTED

Preheat oven to 325° to 350°. Lightly coat a 2-quart casserole dish with nonstick cooking spray.

In medium mixing bowl, combine thawed corn, cream corn, eggs, milk salt, pepper, and cheese. Stir to blend and pour into prepared casserole dish. Sprinkle top with cracker crumbs, if desired. Drizzle melted butter over top and bake for 30 to 35 minutes or until firm, not runny, in the middle.

Makes 8 to 10 servings.

VIRTUALLY ALL THE VEGETABLE DISHES IN THIS BOOK MAY BE ASSEMBLED IN ADVANCE AND REFRIGERATED FOR 1 TO 2 DAYS. BAKE TO FINISH THE DISH JUST BEFORE SERVING. REMOVE FROM REFRIGERATOR 1 HOUR BEFORE PLACING IN OVEN. ADD ABOUT 10 MINUTES BAKING TIME TO HEAT THOROUGHLY.

BAKED WINTER SQUASH

3	LARGE (ABOUT 3–4 POUNDS) ACORN SQUASH, OR OTHER TYPE OF WINTER SQUASH
2	EGGS, LIGHTLY BEATEN
1	CUP BROWN SUGAR (DIVIDED USE)
2	TABLESPOONS FLOUR
1	TEASPOON VANILLA
2	TABLESPOONS BUTTER
½	TEASPOON NUTMEG
½	TEASPOON CINNAMON
1	TEASPOON SALT, OR TO TASTE
½	TEASPOON PEPPER, OR TO TASTE

Preheat oven to 350°. Cut squash in half and scoop out seeds (or strings). Pierce skin side 2 or 3 times with fork.

Place cut-side down on a baking sheet and bake squash until tender and easily pierced with a fork.

Remove from oven, drain, and allow to cool slightly. With an oven mitt, hold squash halves and scoop pulp into a large mixing bowl. You should have about 3 cups. Discard squash shells.

To squash pulp, add eggs, ¾ cup brown sugar, flour, vanilla, butter, nutmeg, cinnamon, salt, and pepper. Using an electric mixer on low speed, blend until smooth. Pour into 2-quart casserole. Sprinkle remaining ¼ cup brown sugar on top. Bake for 30 minutes or until slightly brown around edges.

Makes 8 to 10 servings.

EASY SPINACH CASSEROLE

3	(10-OUNCE) PACKAGES FROZEN CHOPPED SPINACH
2	TABLESPOONS BUTTER
½	CUP ONION, CHOPPED FINE
½	CUP FRESHLY GRATED PARMESAN CHEESE (DIVIDED USE)
1	CUP SOUR CREAM
1	TEASPOON SALT, OR TO TASTE
½	TEASPOON PEPPER, OR TO TASTE

Preheat oven to 325°–350°. Cook spinach according to package directions and drain well, pressing with back of spoon to remove excess liquid.

Combine butter and onion in medium saucepan. Cook until onion is soft. Remove from heat. Stir in spinach, all but 2 tablespoons Parmesan cheese, sour cream, salt and pepper to taste; mixing well. Pour into 1½-quart casserole dish. Sprinkle with remaining Parmesan cheese. Cover with foil and bake for 25 to 30 minutes or until light brown and bubbly.

Makes 8 to 10 servings.

CARROTS *in* CREAM

1	POUND BABY CARROTS
¼	CUP CREAM
½	TEASPOON SALT, OR TO TASTE
¼	TEASPOON PEPPER, OR TO TASTE
½	TEASPOON SUGAR, OR TO TASTE

In medium saucepan, combine carrots and 1 cup cold water. Place over high heat and bring water to a boil. Reduce heat, cover pan, and cook carrots until tender and easily pierced with a fork, about 10 to 15 minutes.

Drain carrots and rinse with cold water to stop the cooking. If desired, refrigerate until serving time.

In same saucepan, combine cream, salt, pepper, and sugar over medium heat. Cook and stir until sugar melts. Add drained carrots, stirring to coat evenly. Heat through and adjust seasoning to taste.

Makes 8 to 10 servings.

CRISPY GREEN BEANS *with* LEMON BROWN BUTTER

1	(16-OUNCE) PACKAGE WHOLE GREEN BEANS, OR 1 POUND POLE BEANS (NOT KENTUCKY WONDERS), ENDS TRIMMED
3	TABLESPOONS UNSALTED BUTTER
1	TABLESPOON LEMON JUICE
1	TEASPOON SALT, OR TO TASTE
½	TEASPOON PEPPER, OR TO TASTE
1	TEASPOON SUGAR, OPTIONAL

In medium saucepan, cook frozen green beans according to package directions. If using fresh beans, bring 1 quart water to a boil over high heat and stir in beans. Allow water to boil again, reduce heat slightly and cook vigorously until beans are easily pierced with a fork, tender, but not mushy, about 10 minutes.

Drain beans and rinse with cold water to stop cooking. At this point, beans may be refrigerated until serving time.

In medium saucepan, melt butter over medium-high heat. When butter begins to bubble, reduce heat to low and continue cooking until butter turns caramel colored and has brown flecks in it. Remove from heat. Stir in lemon juice, salt and pepper to taste.

Add beans to saucepan, toss to coat evenly and heat through. Adjust seasoning to taste, adding 1 teaspoon sugar, if desired.

Variation

Cook 1 (16-ounce) package frozen broccoli according to package directions, or cook 1 pound fresh broccoli florets, as fresh green beans above, until tender, 6 to 8 minutes. Proceed as above. Add ½ teaspoon grated nutmeg.

Makes 8 servings.

SWEET AND CREAMY
TURNIPS, P. 91

No holiday meal at my German grandmother's was complete without turnips. With enough sugar, a requisite for traditional Texas vegetable cooking, turnips can taste milder and softer than you think.

SWEET *and* CREAMY TURNIPS

2	POUNDS TURNIPS, ABOUT 6
1	CUP CREAM
2	TABLESPOONS BUTTER, MELTED
¼	CUP SUGAR
1	TEASPOON SALT, OR TO TASTE
1	TEASPOON PEPPER, OR TO TASTE
1	TEASPOON NUTMEG
¼	CUP FINELY CHOPPED PARSLEY, OPTIONAL

Preheat oven to 325°–350°.

Peel turnips and cut into eights. Place in a large saucepan with cold water to cover over high heat. When water boils, reduce heat to simmer and cook until turnips are easily pierced with a fork, about 15 minutes.

Drain turnips and place in 2-quart casserole dish. Combine cream, butter, sugar, salt, and pepper. Pour over turnips and toss to evenly coat. Add a bit more cream if needed and adjust seasoning to taste. Sprinkle with nutmeg.

Cover turnips and place in oven until heated through, about 20 minutes. Sprinkle with parsley, if desired.

Makes 8 to 10 servings.

MORE VEGETABLE DISHES

CHRISTMAS SWEETS

There's simply no sweeter time of year. The cookies of the season are as evocative as some of the other symbols: the decorated tree, garlands of greenery, and nativity scenes. Cakes, candies, and other desserts are also a big part of the holiday celebration. For some Texans, the memory of the big finale to the family dinner is as memorable as the first bike under the tree.

COOKIES

Cookies are the currency for one of the most traditional of holiday exchanges. The baking of family favorites—to offer visitors, including Santa, and to give to friends and neighbors—is a big part of the seasonal celebration in many homes.

THIS simple cookie, called a Mexican Wedding Cookie, is a Texas favorite. An uncomplicated list of ingredients makes for a wonderful holiday mouthful.

MEXICAN WEDDING COOKIES

½	CUP BUTTER, SOFTENED
½	CUP POWDERED SUGAR (DIVIDED USE)
1	CUP FLOUR
1	TEASPOON VANILLA
½	CUP FINELY CHOPPED PECANS

Preheat oven to 300°.

Using an electric mixer, combine the butter and 2 tablespoons powdered sugar, beating at medium speed until smooth and fluffy.

Sift the flour and blend into butter, mixing thoroughly. Stir in vanilla. Form dough into 1-inch balls and place on an ungreased cookie sheet, or use two fingers to flatten slightly.

THE TEXAS HOLIDAY COOKBOOK

Bake for 25 to 30 minutes, or until firm and light golden in color. Cool slightly on a rack. Sift remaining powdered sugar. Roll cookies in sifted powdered sugar while still warm.

Makes about 24 cookies.

THESE simple sugar cookies are easy to make as pressed cookies, or you may want to roll them and cut into holiday shapes. Few memories are as cherished as making cookies with a mother or grandmother and proudly presenting them to the family.

OLD-FASHIONED SUGAR COOKIES

½	CUP VEGETABLE SHORTENING
1	CUP SUGAR
1	EGG, LIGHTLY BEATEN
1	TEASPOON VANILLA
¼	CUP MILK (OR WATER*)
2½	CUPS FLOUR
2	TEASPOONS BAKING POWDER
¼	TEASPOON SALT

USE A BAKING-POWDER CAN FOR A COOKIE CUTTER WHEN MAKING COOKIES FOR MAILING. AFTER BAKING, PACK THEM FOR MAILING IN THE SAME CAN. THE COOKIES WILL SHRINK A BIT DURING BAKING AND FIT IN THE CONTAINER.

COOL COOKIE SHEETS BETWEEN BAKES TO PREVENT DOUGH FROM SPREADING.

DON'T MIX DIFFERENT KINDS OF COOKIES FOR STORAGE BECAUSE THIS TENDS TO MAKE THEM ALL SOGGY.

Preheat oven to 375°. In medium bowl, combine the shortening and the sugar, beating at high speed with an electric mixer. Mixture should be light and fluffy. Add egg and vanilla.

Sift together the flour, baking powder, and salt. Repeat sifting process, then blend sifted ingredients into egg and sugar mixture.

Chill dough for 1 to 2 hours for easier handling.

Simple Cookies

Roll dough into 1-inch balls. Place balls on an ungreased cookie sheet 2 inches apart. Press each ball with the bottom of a glass that has been dipped in sugar until cookie is about ¼-inch thick. Dip glass in sugar before flattening each cookie. Sprinkle lightly with ground nutmeg or cinnamon. If desired, place a perfect pecan half in the center of each. Bake 8 to 10 minutes or until light golden around the edges. Remove from oven and allow to cool until cookies begin to firm up. Remove to a rack to cool completely.

Cut-Out Cookies

Break off a third to a fourth of the dough, returning the rest to the refrigerator. Place on a lightly floured board and gently roll to ¼-inch thickness. Using holiday cutters, cut cookies into desired shapes. Using a spatula, carefully transfer to ungreased baking sheet. Decorate as desired with sprinkles or other holiday decorations. Bake 8 to 10 minutes or until light golden around the edges. Remove from oven and allow to cool until cookies begin to firm up. Remove to a rack to cool completely. Decorate as desired with Decorator Frosting for Cookies, other icing (homemade or purchased), colored sugar, or other cookie decorations.

Makes 2½ to 3 dozen cookies.

DECORATOR FROSTING *for* COOKIES

½   CUP POWDERED SUGAR

2   TEASPOONS UNSALTED BUTTER
     (OR MARGARINE*), SOFTENED

2   TEASPOONS MILK (OR WATER*)

In small bowl, combine powdered sugar, butter, and milk. Beat at medium speed until smooth. Color as desired with food coloring. Pipe or spread on completely cooled cookies. After decorating, let stand until frosting is set. Store in loosely covered container.

Jewish dietary law forbids dairy and meat in the same meal. To serve these cookies with brisket Hanukkah menu, use non-dairy substitutes.

THESE are similar to mini-pecan pie slices—so good and so festive on a Christmas cookie tray.

PECAN DIAMONDS

½	CUP BUTTER, SOFTENED
¼	CUP GRANULATED SUGAR
3	EGGS (DIVIDED USE)
1 ½	TEASPOONS VANILLA (DIVIDED USE)
1 ¼	CUPS ALL-PURPOSE FLOUR (SIFT BEFORE MEASURING)
⅛	PLUS ½ TEASPOON SALT (DIVIDED USE)
1 ½	CUPS BROWN SUGAR
1	CUP CHOPPED PECANS
2	TABLESPOONS ALL-PURPOSE FLOUR
½	TEASPOON BAKING POWDER

Preheat oven to 350°. Grease a 9 x 12-inch baking pan.

In a small bowl, combine butter and sugar, beating on high speed with an electric mixer until light and fluffy. Beat in 1 egg and ½ teaspoon vanilla.

Add sifted flour and ⅛ teaspoon salt, in 3 parts, mixing with a spoon or on low speed after each addition.

Using your hands, pat the dough evenly into the prepared pan. Bake about 15 minutes, or until crust is light golden.

Meanwhile, lightly beat 2 eggs in a medium bowl. Add brown sugar, stirring to dissolve. Stir in pecans, 2 tablespoons flour, baking powder, ½ teaspoon salt and 1 teaspoon vanilla. Spread over crust and return to oven for about 25 minutes.

Remove from oven and cool completely. Cut into 2 x 2-inch diamond shapes or 1 x 2-inch bars.

Makes about 3 to 4 dozen.

THESE German Ginger Snaps have a touch of pepper, like the other classic winter cookie, *Pfeffernuesse*.

GINGER SNAPS

2	CUPS FLOUR
1	TEASPOON GINGER
1	TEASPOON BAKING POWDER
1	TEASPOON BAKING SODA
¼	TEASPOON BLACK PEPPER
¼	TEASPOON SALT
¾	CUP SHORTENING
1	CUP SUGAR
¼	CUP MOLASSES
1	EGG, LIGHTLY BEATEN

Preheat oven to 375°. Lightly grease cookie sheet(s).

Sift together flour, ginger, baking powder, baking soda, black pepper, and salt. Set aside.

In a large bowl, combine shortening and sugar, beating on high speed with an electric mixer until light and fluffy. Stir in molasses and egg. Blend sifted mixture into creamed mixture, in 3 parts. Stir in or use mixer on low speed. Cover dough and refrigerate for at least an hour, preferably 2 to 3 hours.

Form 1-inch balls and roll in granulated sugar. Place on lightly greased cookie sheet about 2 inches apart. Flatten with the bottom of a glass dipped in sugar to about ¼-inch thick.

If desired, divide dough and roll a portion on lightly floured board ¼-inch thick and cut with cutters, such as classic gingerbread boys or girls. Repeat, using remaining dough. Refrigerate unused portion until ready to shape.

Bake 8 to 10 minutes, or until golden around edges. Remove from pans immediately and cool on wire racks.

Makes about 5 dozen cookies.

ONE of Texans' favorite flavors is that of the margarita, the lime-based cocktail with salt on the rim of the glass. These cookies, with just a touch of (optional) tequila and orange liqueur, may become one of your holiday traditions after you taste one. But don't just think of them at Christmas. They're a natural for New Year's or with Mexican food, anytime you want a light, refreshing cookie.

MARGARITA BALLS

1	(12-OUNCE) PACKAGE VANILLA WAFERS
½	CUP PRETZEL CRUMBS (ABOUT 1 CUP PRETZELS)
1	(16-OUNCE) PACKAGE CONFECTIONERS' SUGAR, SIFTED
¾	CUP FROZEN MARGARITA OR LIMEADE CONCENTRATE, THAWED
2	(3-OUNCE) PACKAGES CREAM CHEESE
1	TEASPOON TEQUILA, OR TO TASTE, OPTIONAL
1	TEASPOON TRIPLE SEC (ORANGE LIQUEUR), OR TO TASTE, OPTIONAL
	RIND FROM 1 LIME, GRATED FINE (DIVIDED USE)
1	(2.25-OUNCE) SHAKER GREEN DECORATOR SUGAR
1	CUP GRANULATED SUGAR

Place half the vanilla wafers in bowl of food processor fitted with knife blade. Process to fine crumbs. Remove crumbs and reserve. Repeat with remaining wafers.

Add pretzels (about 1 cup) to food processor and process to fine crumbs to make ½ cup crumbs.

In a large bowl, combine wafer crumbs, pretzel crumbs, powdered sugar, margarita concentrate, and cream cheese in a large bowl. Add tequila and Triple Sec, if desired. Stir until blended. Divide mixture in half. Wrap each half tightly in plastic and set aside.

Combine half the grated lime with decorator sugar and half with granulated sugar on small saucers or in small bowls, stirring to distribute lime peel evenly.

Remove plastic from 1 portion of the dough and shape into 1-inch balls. After shaping each ball, roll each in green or white sugar. Work quickly, because balls dry quickly. Repeat until all dough is used. Store in an airtight container in refrigerator up to 1 week.

Makes 7 dozen.

MARGARITA BALLS, P. 98

WHEN you want a perfect recipe for kids, try Gail Hearn Plummer's Cinnamon Fingers. Little fingers love to shape the dough into "fingers." And they're virtually impossible to mess up. Besides, they taste great. (They're easy enough for adults to make, too.)

CINNAMON FINGERS

1	CUP UNSALTED BUTTER (2 STICKS), SOFTENED
5	TABLESPOONS GRANULATED SUGAR
2	CUPS ALL-PURPOSE FLOUR (SIFT AFTER MEASURING)
1	TEASPOON VANILLA
½	CUP SUGAR
¼	TEASPOON CINNAMON, OR TO TASTE

SHORTCUT. COMBINE BUTTER, SUGAR, AND FLOUR IN WORK BOWL OF A FOOD PROCESSOR. PROCESS IN SHORT ON-OFF PULSES UNTIL MIXTURE IS CRUMBLY. TRANSFER TO A LARGE BOWL.

Preheat oven to 350°. Combine butter, sugar, and flour in a large bowl. Using a pastry blender, cut in ingredients until mixture is crumbly. Add vanilla and mix with hands to form a smooth dough.

Shape dough into "pinky fingers," about ½-inch wide and 2-inches long.

Place fingers on an ungreased cookie sheet and bake 10 to 12 minutes, just until edges turn golden. Be careful not to overbake.

Meanwhile, combine sugar and cinnamon, mixing well to distribute cinnamon evenly. Place on a small saucer.

After removing fingers from oven, roll in cinnamon sugar to coat evenly. Allow to cool on a wire rack.

Makes 2½ dozen.

ONE TIME MY KIDS WERE MAKING THESE AND DECIDED TO TRY MAKING ONE BIG ONE (ABOUT THE SIZE OF A GILA MONSTER). IT DIDN'T BAKE THE SAME AS THE LITTLE ONES, BUT THEY SURE HAD FUN.

Gail Hearn Plummer

CAKES, CANDIES, PIES *and* DESSERTS

Besides cookies, Christmas is a time for cakes, candies, and pies. Desserts sometimes seem like a main course. Many cooks spend hours, even days, making sweet treats for the holiday season. Nowhere is the influence of German immigrants more evident than in some of Texans' favorite cakes, particularly at Christmas.

(CLOCKWISE FROM TOP) GERMAN CHOCOLATE CAKE, P. 102; TEXAS SHEET CAKE, P. 107; CHOCOLATE CHESS PIE, P. 113

THIS was a chocolate favorite at my German grandmother's house for Christmas. Next to her angel food cake, this was one of her best.

GERMAN CHOCOLATE CAKE *with* COCONUT-PECAN FROSTING

1	(4-OUNCE) BAR SWEET BAKING CHOCOLATE
½	CUP BOILING WATER
1	CUP BUTTER OR MARGARINE, SOFTENED
2	CUPS SUGAR
4	EGGS, SEPARATED
1	TEASPOON VANILLA
2½	CUPS SIFTED CAKE FLOUR (SIFT BEFORE MEASURING)
½	TEASPOON SALT
1	CUP BUTTERMILK

Preheat oven to 350°. Grease bottom and side of 3 (8- or 9-inch) cake pans. Line bottom of pans with round of wax paper.

Off heat, add chocolate to boiling water. Stir until chocolate melts. Allow to cool slightly.

Combine butter and sugar in a large bowl beating on high speed with an electric mixer until light and fluffy. Add egg yolks, one at a time, mixing well after each addition. Blend in chocolate and vanilla, mixing well.

Stir together flour, salt, and soda. Add to chocolate mixture, alternately with buttermilk, beginning and ending with dry ingredients. Beat until smooth.

Beat egg whites until stiff peaks form. Gently, blend about ¼ of the chocolate batter into the egg whites. Then fold egg whites into the remaining batter. Blend gently until uniform color is achieved.

Divide batter evenly in prepared cake pans. Bake for 30 to 40 minutes or until a toothpick inserted in center comes out clean. Cool in pans on rack for 10 minutes, then turn out and cool completely on rack.

COCONUT PECAN FROSTING

1	CUP EVAPORATED MILK (NOT SWEETENED CONDENSED MILK)
1	CUP SUGAR
3	EGG YOLKS, LIGHTLY BEATEN
½	CUP UNSALTED BUTTER
1	TEASPOON VANILLA
1 ½	CUPS FLAKED COCONUT
1	CUP CHOPPED PECANS

Combine evaporated milk, sugar, egg yolks, and butter in a medium saucepan over medium heat. Cook and stir for 12 minutes, or until mixture thickens.

Remove from heat and stir in coconut and pecans. Using a wooden spoon, beat vigorously until mixture is thick enough to spread, about 5 minutes. (Rest your arm when necessary.)

Place 1 chocolate layer on cake plate. Spread thin layer of frosting on top. Add second layer and spread with another thin layer of frosting. Add third layer and spread frosting on top and sides.

Makes 12 to 16 servings.

GROWING UP IN OUR GERMAN COMMUNITY, I REMEMBER HAVING CAKE AND COFFEE IN THE AFTERNOON—ABOUT 4. OFTEN, THE WOMEN WOULD GET TOGETHER AND COMPARE CAKE RECIPES. BEING A GOOD BAKER IS AN IMPORTANT SOCIAL SKILL.

Dorothy Koch Griffith

MADE as a year-round treat for afternoon coffee, this German-style coffee cake has particular personal significance because it was always waiting warm when we arrived on Christmas Eve at my grandmother's house.

It is also wonderful on a holiday morning.

OLGA'S COFFEE CAKE

1	PACKAGE DRY YEAST
¼	CUP LUKEWARM WATER
¾	CUP MILK
½	CUP PLUS 6 TABLESPOONS SUGAR
¼	CUP UNSALTED BUTTER
1	EGG, LIGHTLY BEATEN
1	TEASPOON SALT
3	CUPS FLOUR
3–4	TABLESPOONS MELTED BUTTER

Dissolve yeast in warm water, stirring to activate. Set aside. Heat milk until almost boiling; remove from heat. Add ½ cup sugar and ¼ cup butter. Stir to melt and allow mixture to cool to lukewarm, cool enough not to kill the yeast action nor cook the egg. Transfer to a medium mixing bowl.

Add dissolved yeast, egg, and salt to the lukewarm milk mixture. Add flour, 1 cup at a time, mixing well after each addition. Turn out the dough onto lightly floured board. Knead for 5 to 10 minutes until smooth and no longer sticky. If needed, add a bit more flour.

Place the dough in a lightly greased bowl, cover, and let rise in a warm place until doubled in bulk, about 1½ to 2 hours.

Punch down dough and knead gently in bowl. Allow to rest for 5 to 10 minutes.

Divide dough into 3 pieces. Place on lightly floured board and roll out each piece into a circle about ¼-inch thick and 8 to 9 inches in diameter. Place in a greased 8- or 9-inch cake pan. Cover and let rise again until doubled, about 45 to 60 minutes.

Preheat oven to 375°.

Using fingers, make 6 to 8 indentations in top of each cake. Brush top of cakes with melted butter, allowing butter to puddle in each indention. Sprinkle about 1 tablespoon sugar over top of each cake.

Bake 20 to 25 minutes or until dough begins to brown around the edges. Serve warm or at room temperature.

Makes 3 (8- or 9-inch) coffee cakes.

ALTHOUGH probably English in origin, Coconut Cake has long been associated with a Southern Christmas. In some homes, the holiday wouldn't be the same without a towering white layer cake with frothy coconut icing.

COCONUT CAKE

3½	CUPS SIFTED CAKE FLOUR (SIFT BEFORE MEASURING)
4	TEASPOONS BAKING POWDER
½	PLUS ⅛ TEASPOON SALT
1	CUP UNSALTED BUTTER, SOFTENED
2	CUPS SIFTED SUGAR (SIFT BEFORE MEASURING)
½	CUP MILK PLUS ½ CUP COCONUT MILK, OR 1 CUP MILK
2	TEASPOONS VANILLA (DIVIDED USE)
10	EGG WHITES (DIVIDED USE)
1½	CUPS SUGAR (UNSIFTED)
½	TEASPOON CREAM OF TARTAR
⅓	CUP WATER
2	CUPS (3.5-OUNCE CAN) SHREDDED COCONUT

Preheat oven to 350°. Grease and flour 3 (8- or 9-inch) cake pans.

Combine flour with baking powder and ½ teaspoon salt. Sift together twice.

Place butter in large mixing bowl. Beat at high speed with electric mixer until butter is creamy. Gradually add sugar, beating after each addition. Beat until mixture is light and fluffy.

Add the flour mixture to the butter mixture, alternating with milk/coconut milk, beginning and ending with flour mixture. Add 1 teaspoon vanilla and mix on medium speed until smooth.

Beat 8 egg whites on high speed until stiff peaks form. Gently stir about ¼ of the batter into beaten egg whites. Fold blended egg whites into remaining batter, being careful not to deflate egg whites.

Divide batter between prepared cake pans. Bake about 20 to 23 minutes or until toothpick inserted in center comes out clean.

Allow to cool slightly then invert cake pans on rack and remove pans. Cool cake layers completely before frosting.

To Make Frosting

Combine 1½ cups sugar, cream of tartar, water, and ⅛ teaspoon salt in large saucepan over medium heat. Cook and stir until sugar is dissolved and mixture boils rapidly. Remove from heat. Begin beating syrup mixture at high speed with an electric mixer. Add remaining 2 egg whites in an even stream, beating constantly. Beat until peaks form. Add 1 teaspoon vanilla and continue beating until stiff enough to hold stiff peaks.

Place 1 layer on cake pan. Spread with thin layer of frosting. Sprinkle with ¼ to ⅓ cup shredded coconut. Add second layer and repeat frosting and coconut. Add third layer and frost top and sides with remaining icing. Cover top and sides with remaining coconut.

Makes 12 to 16 servings.

JUST about every region has a version of this cake, but wherever you go, you'll likely find it called the Texas Sheet Cake. Fine, we'll take credit for this easy snack cake that is ideal for the Christmas season.

TEXAS SHEET CAKE

2	CUPS SUGAR
2	CUPS UNBLEACHED FLOUR
½	CUP MARGARINE
½	CUP SHORTENING
¼	CUP COCOA
1	CUP WATER
½	CUP BUTTERMILK
2	EGGS, LIGHTLY BEATEN
1	TEASPOON BAKING SODA
1	TEASPOON VANILLA

Preheat oven to 400°. Grease a 15½ x 10½-inch jelly roll pan.

Sift together sugar and flour in a large bowl. Combine margarine, shortening, cocoa, and water in a saucepan over high heat and bring to a boil. Stir to melt margarine and shortening, remove from heat, and pour over dry ingredients, mixing well.

Allow to cool slightly and stir in buttermilk, eggs, baking soda, and vanilla, mixing well.

Pour batter into prepared pan and bake 20 minutes. Do not overbake. Cake should have a fudge-like texture.

Five minutes before cake is done, prepare the icing.

Icing

½	CUP MARGARINE
¼	CUP COCOA
⅓	CUP MILK
1	POUND POWDERED SUGAR
1	TEASPOON VANILLA
1	CUP CHOPPED PECANS

Combine margarine, cocoa, and milk in medium saucepan. Cook over low heat until margarine is melted.

Allow liquid to boil. Remove from heat. Add powdered sugar, vanilla, and pecans and beat until icing is smooth and sugar is dissolved. Spread over hot cake as soon as it comes out of the oven, while it is still in the pan.

Makes 15 (3-inch) squares.

TEXAS SHEET CAKE, P. 107

TEXAS is the fruitcake capital of the Western World. The granddaddy of them all, the Collin Street Bakery in Corsicana, as well as Eilenberger Bakery (Butternut Baking Co.) in Palestine and Mary of Puddin Hill in Greenville form the Fruitcake Triangle of East Texas. More fruitcakes are baked here than just about any place else you can think of.

With all these fruitcakes to choose from, why even consider baking your own? Because it's Christmas. But you don't have to make a whole fruitcake. For a taste, you can make fruitcake nibbles. Like the Pecan Cake from Eilenberger Bakery (Butternut Baking Co.) in Palestine, they're heavy on nuts, lighter on candied fruit.

FRUITCAKE NIBBLES

¾	CUP SUGAR
¼	CUP UNSALTED BUTTER, SOFTENED
1	EGG
1⅓	CUPS SIFTED FLOUR (SIFT BEFORE MEASURING)
¼	TEASPOON CINNAMON
¼	TEASPOON NUTMEG
¼	TEASPOON GROUND CLOVES
¼	TEASPOON SALT
½	TEASPOON BAKING SODA
1	CUP COARSELY CHOPPED PECANS
½	CUP DRIED OR CANDIED FRUIT, CHOPPED
2	TABLESPOONS BRANDY OR BOURBON

Preheat oven to 350°. Grease and flour three baking sheets or allow sheet to cool between batches. Grease and flour baking sheet each time before forming cookies.

In a medium mixing bowl, beat together sugar, butter, and egg. Sift flour, cinnamon, nutmeg, cloves, baking soda, and salt into bowl. Mix by hand until blended. Add nuts, fruit and brandy or bourbon. Stir to blend. Batter will be stiff.

Drop dough by rounded teaspoonfuls onto baking sheet. Bake for 12 to 15 minutes, or until golden, about 1 inch apart. If desired, line miniature muffin cups with muffin liners and fill three-quarters full.

Makes about 3 dozen cookies.

THE yin and yang of Texas Christmas candy are chocolate fudge and divinity. With or without nuts, usually pecans, divinity, as white and fluffy as fudge is dark and dense, is the perfect yang to chocolate's yin. A true Texas holiday candy-maker does both.

Chocolate Fudge

2½	CUPS SUGAR
½	CUP UNSALTED BUTTER
¼	TEASPOON SALT
1	(5-OUNCE) CAN EVAPORATED MILK (NOT SWEETENED CONDENSED MILK), ABOUT ⅔ CUP
1	(7-OUNCE) JAR MARSHMALLOW CREME, ABOUT 2 CUPS
1	(12-OUNCE) PACKAGE SEMISWEET CHOCOLATE CHIPS, ABOUT 2 CUPS
¾	CUP FINELY CHOPPED PECANS
1	TEASPOON VANILLA
½	TEASPOON BOURBON, OPTIONAL

Line a 9-inch square pan with foil so that foil extends over the sides of the pan. Rub foil with butter.

Combine sugar, butter, salt, and evaporated milk in a 2-quart microwave-safe bowl. A large glass measuring bowl, with a handle works particularly well. Microwave on High for 6 to 8 minutes, or until mixture comes to a rolling boil, stirring twice.

Add marshmallow creme and chocolate chips; blend until smooth. Stir in pecans, vanilla, and bourbon, if desired. Pour into buttered, foil-lined pan. Cool to room temperature. Using the tip of a knife, mark the fudge into 36 squares. Refrigerate until firm.

To remove fudge from pan, lift foil from pan. Remove foil from sides of fudge. Cut through the lines to make 36 pieces. Store fudge in refrigerator.

Conventional Directions

Prepare pan as above. Combine sugar, butter, salt, and evaporated milk in a large saucepan over medium heat. Bring to a boil, stirring constantly. Boil 5 minutes, stirring constantly. Remove from heat. Add remaining ingredients and proceed as above.

Variation

For White Chocolate Fudge, substitute white chocolate chips for semisweet chocolate chips. Proceed as above.
Makes 36 pieces.

DIVINITY

2¾	CUPS SUGAR (DIVIDED USE)
¾	CUP WHITE CORN SYRUP
¼	CUP WATER
2	EGG WHITES
1	TEASPOON VANILLA
1	CUP COARSELY CHOPPED PECANS

Combine 2½ cups sugar, corn syrup, and water in a saucepan over medium heat. Bring to a boil, stirring constantly. When mixture boils, continue cooking at a boil and without stirring until mixture reaches 250° on a candy thermometer. Remove from heat.

Place egg whites in medium bowl. With electric mixer, begin beating egg whites. When egg whites are foamy, gradually add ¼ cup sugar, beating continuously until egg whites form stiff peaks. Pour the boiled mixture slowly into the egg whites, beating constantly on high speed with electric beaters. Stir in vanilla and chopped pecans.

Working quickly, drop candy by teaspoonfuls onto wax paper and cool. Store in air-tight containers.
Makes 3½ dozen.

THIS CONFECTION CAN BE TRICKY ON HUMID DAYS. THE CANDY JUST WON'T "SET UP," OR FIRM ENOUGH TO HOLD A SHAPE. NEVER MIND IF IT FLATTENS TO LITTLE PATTIES. GIVE IT A DAY TO DRY OUT, THEN SHAPE THE PATTIES INTO MOUNDS. THEY'LL BE JUST FINE.

You've probably enjoyed pralines in Tex-Mex restaurants. There's usually a platterful at the cash register. So rich, so monstrous, so chockful of nuts, you wonder why they're the perfect ending to a meal as big as an Enchilada Special. No one knows why. They just are. And they're also very much a Texas tradition at Christmas, for giving or having on hand.

PRALINES

2	CUPS SUGAR
¾	CUP MILK
½	TEASPOON BAKING SODA
1	TEASPOON VANILLA
1	TEASPOON BUTTER
1 ½	CUPS SHELLED PECAN HALVES OR BROKEN PECAN PIECES

In a large saucepan, combine sugar, milk, and baking soda. Cook over high heat, stirring constantly. Bring mixture to a boil. Continue boiling and stirring until it reaches 240° on a candy thermometer (soft-ball stage).

Remove from heat and add butter, vanilla, and pecans. Using a wooden spoon, beat until mixture begins to hold a shape. Drop by tablespoonfuls onto lightly greased or buttered wax paper.

Makes 1½ dozen.

GAIL HEARN PLUMMER is famous at her family reunions in the Hill Country for her Chocolate Chess Pie. It is a "must" for her Christmas table, but draws raves any time of year.

CHOCOLATE CHESS PIE

2	CUPS SUGAR (SIFT AFTER MEASURING)
1	TABLESPOON CORNMEAL
¼	CUP COCOA
1	TABLESPOON FLOUR
1	TEASPOON SALT
4	EGGS, WELL-BEATEN
½	CUP MILK
1	TEASPOON VANILLA
½	CUP MELTED BUTTER
1	CUP CHOPPED PECANS
1	(9-INCH) PASTRY FOR SINGLE CRUST PIE, UNBAKED

Preheat oven to 350°. Combine sifted sugar, cornmeal, cocoa, flour, and salt in a large mixing bowl. Stir to mix. Add eggs, milk, vanilla, and butter. Stir until smooth.

Blend in pecans. Pour filling into unbaked crust. Place in oven and bake for 1 hour or until filling is set and crust is golden. If crust begins to brown too fast, lower oven to 325° and place a ring of foil over the crust.

Makes 8 servings.

CHOCOLATE CHESS PIE IS A MUST FOR MY FAMILY AT CHRISTMAS. EVERYONE ALWAYS ASKS FOR IT. BUT THIS IS WHAT I SERVE ANYTIME I WANT SOMETHING PEOPLE WILL JUST GO CRAZY OVER.

Gail Hearn Plummer

My very German grandmother (Olga Reichle Koch, we called her Mo-Mo) on my mother's side and my very Southern grandmother (Netta Morrill Griffith, we called her Netsie Mother) on my dad's side had at least one thing in common around Christmas: mincemeat pie with egg nog. Again, this is likely an English tradition via the Old South.

I can't say the pie was my favorite as a kid, but it was a custom that insinuated itself into the celebrations of those two families from very different backgrounds.

Both relied on prepared mincemeat, which, in contemporary preparations, doesn't contain any meat. It is raisins, dates, and similar dried fruit. It is something grandmothers love.

MINCE-APPLE PIE

3	CUPS APPLE, PEELED AND SLICED
¼	CUP SUGAR
1	TABLESPOON FLOUR
1	(28-OUNCE) JAR PREPARED MINCEMEAT
3	TABLESPOONS BOURBON, BRANDY, OR ORANGE JUICE
	PASTRY FOR 2-CRUST PIE, SEE PP. 38–39

Preheat oven to 450°.

Toss together apples, sugar, and flour. Fold into mincemeat, along with bourbon, brandy, or juice.

Line bottom of 9-inch pie plate with bottom crust. Fill with mincemeat filling. Cover the pie with a layer of pastry. Seal and flute edges. Prick top with fork. Decorate as desired with pastry.

Bake for 10 minutes, then lower heat to 350°. Bake about 30 minutes longer, until pastry is golden.

Serve warm with dollop of vanilla ice cream, or at room temperature with whipped cream.

Makes 8 servings.

WHILE tamales are almost always present on holiday tables in households with Mexican origins, a special kind of tamale shows up at Christmas: the Sweet Tamale. The tamale dough is flavored with cinnamon and sugar, then it is filled with pecans and raisins. Sweet Tamales are particularly good with hot chocolate.

SWEET TAMALES

5	CUPS MASA HARINA (FOUND ALONGSIDE FLOUR AND CORNMEAL IN THE SUPERMARKET)
2	TEASPOONS SALT, OR TO TASTE
1	TEASPOON BAKING POWDER
1	TABLESPOON CINNAMON
½	CUP SUGAR
1	CUP LARD (NO SUBSTITUTES)
3	CUPS (APPROXIMATELY) CHICKEN STOCK, HEATED
⅔	CUP PECANS, COARSELY CHOPPED
¾	CUP RAISINS
3	DOZEN CORN HUSKS, RINSED AND SOAKED IN HOT WATER FOR SEVERAL HOURS TO SOFTEN

To Prepare the Dough

Combine masa harina, salt, baking powder, cinnamon and sugar; set aside. Place lard in a large mixing bowl and beat at high speed with an electric beater until light and fluffy, about 3 to 5 minutes. Add masa mixture in 2 to 3 batches,

SWEET TAMALES,
SEE RECIPE ABOVE

alternately with the warm (not hot) broth, beating constantly. Add nuts, mixing to distribute evenly through the dough.

Dough should be soft, but pliable, not watery. To test dough, place a small piece in a cup of water. If the dough floats, it is the right consistency.

To Shape and Wrap Tamales

Pat dry the corn husks. Wet your hands. Place a husk in the palm of one hand, and using the back of a spoon, spread about 2 tablespoons of the dough into a rectangle, starting at the wide end of the shuck. Leave about 1½ inches at the wide end of the shuck and about 3 inches at the pointed end. Spread dough to within ¾-inch of the sides.

Fill with 1 teaspoon raisins. Roll sides of tamales to seal the filling. Fold over wide end to seal bottom. Place folded side down on cookie sheet or large sheet of foil. Repeat until dough and filling are used. You should have about 2 dozen.

To Steam

Use a large tamale steamer or large pot with a rack or colander in the bottom. Fill bottom with water to depth of about 1 inch. Water should not touch the rack. Line rack with some of the remaining shucks. Arrange tamales vertically—wide, folded end down—on rack. Tamales should be packed, but not crammed, so they will remain vertical. Cover the tamales with more corn husks or a layer of clean dish towels to prevent the tamales from absorbing too much water. They should be steamed, not immersed. Cover pot with lid.

Bring water to a boil, reduce heat, and simmer for 1½ hours. Make sure water does not cook away during this time; add more as needed. Check tamales for doneness. Tamales are done when the masa easily separates from the husk and the tamale retains its shape. If not done, continue steaming for up to 2½ hours, or as needed. If necessary, cook tamales in batches, reserving tamales in refrigerator until ready to cook.

Cooked tamales may be refrigerated several days or frozen for several weeks. Reheat, wrapped tightly in foil, in a 300° oven, about 30 minutes.

Makes about 2 dozen.

MEXICAN HOT CHOCOLATE

3	(1-OUNCE) SQUARES UNSWEETENED CHOCOLATE
6	CUPS MILK
¼	CUP SUGAR
2	TEASPOONS GROUND CINNAMON
¼	TEASPOON SALT
2	TEASPOONS VANILLA
6	CINNAMON STICKS, OPTIONAL

Using a sharp knife, break up chocolate squares into smaller pieces. In a medium saucepan, combine chocolate, milk, sugar, cinnamon, and salt. Heat and stir until chocolate melts and milk is very hot. Do not allow to boil. Add vanilla and beat until frothy with a rotary beater or with an electric mixer on low speed.

Pour into mugs. Garnish each with a cinnamon stick.

Makes 6 (8-ounce) servings.

MEXICAN HOT CHOCOLATE, SEE RECIPE BELOW, IN TRADITIONAL MUG AND PITCHER WITH A *MOLINILLO*, FOR STIRRING AND FROTHING. SWEET TAMALES, P. 114 AND MEXICAN WEDDING COOKIES, P. 92

TRADITIONALLY, MEXICAN CHOCOLATE IS STIRRED IN A PITCHER OR LARGE MUG WITH A *MOLINILLO*, A DECORATIVELY CARVED WOODEN BEATER RESEMBLING A PESTLE. TWIRLING THE TOOL BETWEEN THE PALMS MAKES FOR A DRAMATIC PRESENTATION.

OTHER Tex-Mex traditions are sweet, such as flan. This caramel custard is a beautiful dessert for any holiday meal.

FLAN

1 ½	CUPS SUGAR (DIVIDED USE)
5	EGGS, WELL-BEATEN
1	(13-OUNCE) CAN EVAPORATED MILK
1	CUP HEAVY CREAM
2	TEASPOONS VANILLA

IT IS EASIER TO CARAMELIZE THE SUGAR IN THE SAME PAN IN WHICH YOU BAKE THE FLAN. USE A 9-INCH CAKE PAN, A TART PAN, OR RING MOLD. THE PAN MUST BE ABLE TO WITHSTAND STOVETOP HEAT. USE HEAVY OVEN MITTS TO HANDLE. YOU MAY ALSO CARAMELIZE THE SUGAR IN A SMALL SAUCEPAN OR SKILLET AND QUICKLY POUR INTO A GLASS PIE PLATE OR PORCELAIN QUICHE PLATE FOR BAKING FLAN.

Sprinkle ½ cup sugar over bottom of a 9-inch cake pan and place over medium heat. Cook, stirring constantly, until sugar melts and turns golden brown. Remove from heat. Turn pan to coat bottom and sides evenly. Allow to cool.

In a medium mixing bowl, combine ¾ cup sugar, eggs, evaporated milk, cream, and vanilla, blending well. Pour over caramel in pan. Place pan with flan in a larger pan.

Place in oven. Pour enough hot water into larger pan to come up the side of flan pan about 1 inch. Bake for 55 to 60 minutes, or until a knife inserted near the center comes out clean. Center will jiggle but not appear fluid.

Remove from oven and lift flan pan from water. Cool for 10 to 15 minutes. Invert onto a serving dish with a rim. The caramel will form a sauce on top of the baked custard.

Variation

May substitute 1 (10-ounce) can sweetened condensed milk and 1 cup milk for evaporated milk and heavy cream. Omit ¾ cup sugar.

Makes 8 servings.

THE punch bowls of England and the hospitality of the Old South bring to mind the rich Christmas beverage we know as eggnog. The most traditional preparation–with a dozen raw eggs–has fallen out of favor in recent years because of concerns about salmonella poisoning.

This version, adapted to use a boiled custard instead of raw eggs, keeps the tradition alive in a tasty and authentic way. It has scant resemblance to commercially prepared eggnog available in refrigerator cases.

With spirits added, this punch is potent. If desired, use less alcohol or none at all.

EGGNOG

⅓	CUP PLUS 3 TABLESPOONS SUGAR
2	EGGS, SEPARATED
¼	TEASPOON SALT
4	CUPS MILK
2	TEASPOONS VANILLA
1	CUP BOURBON, DARK RUM OR BRANDY (OR A COMBINATION TO MAKE 1 CUP), OPTIONAL
½	CUP WHIPPING CREAM
	GROUND NUTMEG

MAKE TWO BATCHES OF EGGNOG, WITH AND WITH-OUT SPIRITS. MAKE SURE GUESTS KNOW THEY HAVE AN OPTION. AS IF THEY COULDN'T TELL AFTER EVEN ONE SIP.

In large saucepan, combine ⅓ cup sugar and egg yolks. Beat until smooth and light yellow in color. Add salt and stir in milk. Cook over medium heat, stirring constantly, until mixture bubbles and thickens enough to coat the back of a spoon.

Remove from heat and stir in vanilla. Place custard in rigid refrigerator container or pitcher with lid. Stir in spirits, if desired. Place a layer of plastic wrap directly on custard. Place lid on container and refrigerate to cool completely, 3 to 4 hours.

Just before serving, whip cream until peaks form. Pour chilled egg nog into a chilled punch bowl and garnish with dollops of whipped cream floating on top. Sprinkle with nutmeg.

Makes 6 to 8 servings.

Variation

Float scoops of vanilla ice cream in eggnog.

NEW YEAR'S

WHILE tradition often dictates the menu on other holidays, superstition is the main ingredient for ringing in a new year. Eating black-eyed peas is as much a requirement for a Texas New Year as rice is for a Chinese New Year.

NEW YEAR'S EVE

New Year's Eve is party time in Texas. Nothing says party in this state like nachos, an assortment of dips, including guacamole, margaritas, and a cooler full of Texas and Mexican beers. If that doesn't make you yearn for a steaming bowl of Menudo on New Year's Day, you won't need it.

Nachos, a snack said to have originated in the border town of Piedras Negras, can be as simple as cheese melted on chips with a slice of jalapeño. Indeed, that is the dish attributed to a waiter named "Nacho." Or nachos can be more elaborate, with a smear of refried beans, and a mouthful of beef or chicken. Garnishes can be many and varied, such as guacamole, sour cream, and Pico de Gallo (see page 155).

Nachos

1	(24-OUNCE) BAG TORTILLA CHIPS
1	(16-OUNCE) PACKAGE GRATED CHEDDAR CHEESE
1	(12-OUNCE) JAR OR CAN SLICED JALAPEÑOS
1	(16-OUNCE) CAN REFRIED BEANS, OPTIONAL
½	POUND GROUND BEEF, COOKED, OPTIONAL
2	CUPS SHREDDED, COOKED CHICKEN, OPTIONAL
1	CUP GUACAMOLE, OPTIONAL (P. 125)
1	CUP SOUR CREAM, OPTIONAL
½	CUP PICO DE GALLO, OPTIONAL (P. 155)
1	CUP RINGS SLICED FROM A LARGE ONION, OPTIONAL

Preheat broiler. Arrange tortilla chips in a single layer on several baking sheets. For basic nachos, top with a sprinkle of grated cheese and a jalapeño slice. If mild nachos are desired, omit some or all of the jalapeño slices and serve as a garnish. Place nachos under broiler just until cheese melts, 3 to 5 minutes.

Options

· Spread each chip with refried beans before topping with cheese and pepper. Proceed as above.

· Cook ground beef in a skillet over medium heat until brown. Drain off fat. Add 1 tablespoon chili powder and 1 tablespoon water, stirring well. Cook 5 minutes longer. Place a teaspoon of ground beef on top of each chip. Top with cheese. Add jalapeños as desired. Proceed as above.

New Year's Day Menu

For killer nachos, make them with the works—some of everything: cheese, jalapeños, beans, beef, chicken, guacamole, sour cream, and Pico de Gallo. Offer plenty of Salsa (p. 154) and Chile con Queso (p. 124), as well. Nachos like that are a meal, not a snack.

SHORTCUTS

- Omit onions. Combine processed cheese with tomatoes and green chilies and chicken stock in a 2-quart microwave-safe dish. Microwave on High for 3 minutes; stir. Continue microwaving, stirring at 1-minute intervals, until cheese is melted.

- Omit onions and chicken stock. Combine processed cheese with undrained tomatoes and green chilies or 1 cup bottled salsa in a 2-quart microwave-safe dish. Follow above instructions for heating in microwave.

· Shred chicken and place a tablespoon on top of each chip. Top with cheese. Add jalapeños as desired. Proceed as above.

· After removing nachos from oven, garnish every other nacho or so with a teaspoon of guacamole, or arrange ¼-cup dollops strategically around nacho platter.

· After removing nachos from oven, garnish every other nacho or so with a teaspoon of sour cream, or arrange ¼-cup dollops strategically around nacho platter.

· After removing nachos from oven, garnish every other nacho or so with a teaspoon of Pico de Gallo, or arrange ¼-cup dollops strategically around nacho platter.

· After removing nachos from oven, garnish with fresh onion rings.

Makes 8 to 10 servings.

Dallas restaurateur Matt Martinez swears the key to a great Chile con Queso is a bit of chicken stock. Believe him. Chicken stock mellows the taste of the cheese and gives it a smoother texture that doesn't get gooey.

Chile con Queso

½	cup onion, coarsely chopped
1	(10-ounce) can tomatoes with green chilies, drained
1	(16-ounce) block of processed cheese, cut in 2-inch cubes
½–¾	cup chicken stock, or as needed (divided use)

Place onion in a large saucepan over low heat. Add 1 tablespoon chicken stock and cook until onion begins to soften, about 5 minutes. Stir in tomatoes and cheese. As cheese begins to melt, stir in chicken stock, ¼ cup at a time, until cheese is melted. Add chicken stock as needed for desired consistency.

Use minimum chicken stock to make a thick sauce for dipping tortilla chips. Add more stock for a thinner consistency to use as a sauce for spooning over other dishes, such as enchiladas.

This recipe reheats with great success.

Makes about 4 cups.

Variations

Brown and drain fat from 1 cup ground beef, bulk pork, or Italian sausage, chorizo (Mexican sausage), or shred 1 cup leftover barbecued brisket or chicken and add to Chile con Queso just before serving.

In Texas, all that's required for a party are two friends, chips, Chile con Queso, and Guacamole. There's simply nothing better.

GUACAMOLE

3	LARGE RIPE AVOCADOS (ABOUT 3 CUPS)
1	CUP PEELED AND CHOPPED TOMATO, DRAINED
½	CUP FINELY CHOPPED ONION
1	TEASPOON SALT, OR TO TASTE
	JUICE OF ½ LEMON OR LIME OR TO TASTE

Peel avocados and place pulp in a medium bowl. Use a fork or potato masher to coarsely mash. Add tomato, onion, salt, and lemon or lime juice. Stir and mash again to desired consistency. Mixture should not be too smooth. Serve immediately as a dip for tortilla chips or as a garnish for nachos or enchiladas.

Makes 3 cups.

SHORTCUTS (CON'T.)

• OMIT ONIONS. COMBINE CHEESE, CHICKEN STOCK, AND DRAINED TOMATOES AND GREEN CHILIES, OR UNDRAINED TOMATOES AND GREEN CHILIES, IN A STOCKPOT. HEAT ON HIGH UNTIL CHEESE MELTS. ADD CHICKEN STOCK IF ADDITIONAL LIQUID IS NEEDED. KEEP WARM ON LOW SETTING.

SHORTCUT. COMBINE MASHED AVOCADO AND ½ CUP BOTTLED SALSA. ADD SALT AND LEMON OR LIME JUICE TO TASTE.

TO KEEP GUACAMOLE FROM TURNING BROWN, RETAIN THE SEEDS AND PLACE IN THE DIP UNTIL SERVING TIME. WHEN GUACAMOLE IS MIXED, PLACE SEEDS IN THE DIP AND COVER TIGHTLY WITH PLASTIC WRAP AND REFRIGERATE. PLACE WRAP DIRECTLY ON DIP TO KEEP OUT AS MUCH AIR AS POSSIBLE.

MOST people think margaritas come from machines. And a lot of them do.

A margarita machine is a pretty typical addition to many parties, at New Year's and other times.

There are also a number of mixes on the market to make margaritas an almost instant drink. All you add is the mix, tequila, and ice to a blender and you've got a frozen margarita. Some margarita mixes even come in tubs. Just pour in tequila and put the tub in the freezer.

But the real thing isn't a frozen drink. It is a cocktail. And the secret isn't the shelf the tequila comes from. The secret to a great margarita is Triple Sec liqueur, an orange flavored liqueur that gives the drink its sparkle.

A REAL MARGARITA

½   CUP FRESH LIME JUICE

½   CUP TEQUILA

½   CUP TRIPLE SEC (ORANGE-FLAVORED) LIQUEUR

     LIME WEDGES

Combine lime juice, tequila, and Triple Sec in a large cocktail shaker or a pitcher with ice. Shake or stir to mix and chill. Strain into chilled cocktail glasses, with or without ice. Garnish with lime wedges.

Optional

Pour 1 cup coarse or kosher salt into a saucer. Rub rim of chilled cocktail glass with lime slice, then dip rim in salt. Pour margarita into glass with salted rim.

Makes 3 servings.

(FROM UPPER LEFT,
CLOCKWISE) GUACAMOLE,
P. 125, AND TORTILLA
CHIPS; SALSA, P. 154;
TEXAS BEER; KILLER
NACHOS, P. 124;
MENUDO, P. 141, WITH
FRESH FLOUR TORTILLA

New Year's Day

For many Texans, football is as much a part of New Year's Day as Thanksgiving Day. Although the Super Bowl isn't played until later in January, many Texans get a head start with a super bowl of Black-Eyed Peas, Chili, Gumbo, or Tortilla Soup. And don't forget the Menudo, if a day-after cure is needed.

Barbecue—beef, ribs, sausage, or a combination—also makes a great spread. It is classic casual food for eating whenever the mood strikes or during commercials. Often barbecue is brought home from a favorite neighborhood smokehouse, but a lot of Texans take pride in their home-made barbecue. For those determined do-it-yourselfers, here's how.

Matt Martinez, who has made it his mission in life to make homemade barbecue about as good as that of the master cookers with the big rigs, developed this technique. It gives a good smoke flavor to the meat without the hassle of minding a smoker. Have ready a squirt gun to douse any flames that might flare when the fat hits the fire.

Barbecue Brisket

1	(8–10-POUND) WHOLE BEEF BRISKET, UNTRIMMED
2	TABLESPOONS GARLIC SALT
2	TABLESPOONS LEMON PEPPER
2	TABLESPOONS PAPRIKA
1	TABLESPOON CHILI POWDER
1	TABLESPOON SUGAR

SHORTCUT. USE YOUR FAVORITE PACKAGED BARBECUE SEASONING MIX OR RUB.

Remove brisket from refrigerator about 1 hour before grilling. Combine garlic salt, lemon pepper, paprika, chili powder, and sugar. Sprinkle over entire surface of meat, concentrating on the fat layer. Rub or press seasoning into meat.

Cover and let meat come to room temperature. Light a fire in a charcoal grill that is big enough to hold the brisket. Allow coals to burn down to gray ash. Place brisket on grill, fat side down.

Grill until fat is charred, turning occasionally when necessary, to stop fat from dripping onto fire. Squirt flareups with water to douse flames.

It will take about 45 minutes to grill the brisket. Remove brisket from grill.

Preheat oven to 300°. Place brisket on a double thickness of foil in a shallow roasting pan. Wrap brisket tightly and bake for 4 to 5 hours, or until meat is very tender. Remove brisket from oven and peel back foil.

Raise oven temperature to 350°. Return brisket to oven and roast, uncovered, for 30 minutes to crisp the top layer of fat.

Allow meat to rest for 20 minutes. Slice across the grain into thin slices. Serve with barbecue sauce.

Makes 10 to 12 servings.

BARBECUE BRISKET, P. 128;
GUACAMOLE, P. 125; AND
PINTO BEANS, P. 134

BARBECUE SAUCE

1 ¼	CUPS KETCHUP
⅓	CUP **WORCESTERSHIRE SAUCE**
⅓	CUP LEMON JUICE
⅓	CUP BROWN SUGAR
⅓	CUP FINELY CHOPPED ONION
1	TABLESPOON YELLOW MUSTARD
¼	CUP WATER
1	CLOVE GARLIC, CRUSHED
¼	CUP PAN DRIPPINGS FROM BARBECUE, OPTIONAL

Combine ketchup, Worcestershire sauce, lemon juice, brown sugar, onion, mustard, water, and garlic in a medium saucepan. Place over very low heat and simmer, stirring occasionally, 1 hour.

Stir in pan drippings and cook 15 minutes longer.

Serve with sliced beef brisket.

SHORTCUT. ADD 2 TO 3 TABLESPOONS BARBECUE PAN DRIPPINGS TO 1 BOTTLE BARBECUE SAUCE. HEAT AND SERVE.

It is easy to forget that a big chunk of Texas is beach, from Louisiana to Mexico. Seafood dishes like Gumbo, especially near the Louisiana border, are an art form every bit as developed as Chili in San Antonio.

GULF GUMBO

⅓	CUP FLOUR
3	TABLESPOONS VEGETABLE OIL
1	CUP CHOPPED ONION
½	CUP GREEN BELL PEPPER, CHOPPED
½	CUP CELERY, CHOPPED
2	CLOVES GARLIC, CRUSHED
1	(28-OUNCE) CAN TOMATOES, CHOPPED (JUICE RESERVED)
6	CUPS CHICKEN STOCK
½	CUP BOTTLED CLAM JUICE OR OYSTER LIQUOR
1	(8-OUNCE) PACKAGE FROZEN SLICED OKRA
½	TEASPOON LEAF OREGANO
1	BAY LEAF
1	TEASPOON BLACK PEPPER
½	TEASPOON CAYENNE PEPPER, OR TO TASTE
1	TEASPOON SALT, OR TO TASTE
1	POUND SEAFOOD: PEELED SHRIMP, CRAB, OR WHITE FISH (SUCH AS SNAPPER OR CATFISH), CUT INTO 1-INCH CUBES (OR A COMBINATION)
12	FRESH OYSTERS, LIQUID RESERVED, OPTIONAL
1	TABLESPOON FILE POWDER
6	CUPS COOKED RICE

Heat vegetable oil in a large pot or Dutch oven over low heat. Stir in flour and cook, stirring constantly, until flour is dark brown, about 30 minutes. Add onions, green pepper, celery and garlic. Cook until vegetables soften and onions begin to brown.

Stir tomatoes and their juice, stock, clam juice, and reserved oyster liquor, if desired, into vegetables.

Add okra, oregano, bay leaf, black pepper, cayenne, and salt. Bring liquid to a boil, reduce heat and simmer, uncovered about 30 minutes until vegetables are tender.

Add seafood and cook just until seafood texture firms, 5 to 10 minutes. Fish will turn white, shrimp will turn pink and oysters will curl.

Adjust seasoning to taste. Just before serving, add file (ground sassafras) to thicken Gumbo to desired consistency. Do not allow liquid to boil again or file will appear stringy and clumpy.

Ladle Gumbo over cooked rice in shallow bowls.

Makes 12 servings.

FOR COOKED RICE. IN A 2-QUART MICROWAVE-SAFE DISH WITH LID, COMBINE 3 CUPS RICE AND 6 CUPS WATER. ADD 2 TEASPOONS SALT. COOK ON HIGH FOR 8 MINUTES OR UNTIL LIQUID BOILS. REDUCE POWER TO MEDIUM AND COOK 25 MINUTES, OR UNTIL RICE IS TENDER AND LIQUID IS ABSORBED. FLUFF WITH A FORK BEFORE SERVING. MAKES 12 SERVINGS.

IT WAS THE NEW YEAR'S I DREADED (MORE THAN 20 YEARS AGO). NEWLY DIVORCED, I WAS STARTING THIS NEW YEAR AS "HALF OF A WHOLE." I HAD PLANS TO BE WITH MY MOTHER ON CHRISTMAS DAY, BUT NOTHING FOR NEW YEAR'S. I DID NOT WANT TO START A NEW BEGINNING IN A MAUDLIN STATE OF MIND. I WANTED TO BE WITH PEOPLE THAT I LIKED AND THOSE WITH WHOM I SHARE THE COMMON GIFT OF LAUGHTER. FINE! IF I HAD NOWHERE TO GO, I WOULD HAVE A PARTY! THE INVITATIONS WENT OUT—"BLACK TIE." THE HUSBANDS DIDN'T MUCH LIKE THE IDEA OF STIFF COLLARS, BUT THE WIVES LOVED IT. NEW YEAR'S EVE AT MY HOUSE—A PARTY OF "NINE." THE MENU READ: VICHYSSOISE, SOLE VERONIQUE, FILET OF BEEF TENDERLOIN WITH TOMATOES RICHELIEU, ROASTED POTATO BALLS, GINGERED PEAS, AND WALNUT TORTE. THAT NEW YEAR'S EVE WAS A MILESTONE: I REALIZED THAT ONE CAN BE A WHOLE NUMBER. FINE DRESS, FINE FRIENDS, FINE FRENCH FOOD. BUT IN THE SPIRIT OF TEXAS, I BOILED THE POTATOES FOR THE VICHYSSOISE WITH A GREAT BIG HAM HOCK.

Suzie Humphreys

A "MESS O'GREENS" is another holiday tradition for many Texans. Sometimes you'll find greens on a Thanksgiving or Christmas table. They're also wonderful with a spread, including ham, smoked turkey, or barbecue, on New Year's Day.

A BIG POT *of* GREENS

3	BUNCHES OF TURNIP, COLLARD, OR MUSTARD GREENS (OR A COMBINATION)
3–4	DRIED SMALL, RED PEPPERS
1–2	CUPS CHICKEN STOCK OR WATER
¼	POUND SALT PORK, OPTIONAL
1–2	TABLESPOONS SUGAR, OPTIONAL

Tear off thick stems and place greens in the sink. Cover with water. Sprinkle a small amount of salt over greens and stir. Allow water to settle a few minutes. Carefully lift out greens and place in a colander or large bowl. (If you have a double sink, the other side works great.)

Rinse out sink to eliminate any grit that may have dropped from greens. Return greens to sink and cover with water again. Allow any remaining grit to settle and unplug drain so that water runs out.

Tear large leaves into pieces and place in a large stockpot, Dutch oven or saucepan with a lid. Without shaking off too much water, add greens to pan, along with whole, dried red peppers.

It may be difficult to get all the greens in the pan, but cram them in. Cover pan with lid and place over medium heat. Cook just until leaves wilt and greens fit easily into pan.

Add just enough water or chicken stock to almost cover greens. If desired, add salt pork. Bring liquid to a boil, reduce heat and simmer until greens are tender, about 30 minutes. Stir in sugar during last 10 minutes of cooking.

Makes 10 servings.

Chili and Tamales (p. 32) are another flavor-intense combination for the day after. Chili is just as good served with a handful of crackers, tortilla chips, warm corn or flour tortillas or cornbread (p. 138). Notice there are no beans in the chili recipe below. In Texas, beans are something you serve with chili as an option. Those that want beans with Chili can add them. Chili is also great over rice with grated cheese and finely chopped onions.

Chili con Carne

3	POUNDS COARSELY GROUND BEEF OR VENISON, OR A MIXTURE (DIVIDED USE)
4	CLOVES GARLIC, CRUSHED
7	TABLESPOONS CHILI POWDER (DIVIDED USE)
1	TABLESPOON GROUND CUMIN
1	(8-OUNCE) CAN TOMATO SAUCE
2	CUPS WATER, OR AS NEEDED
3	TABLESPOONS MASA HARINA OR INSTANT DISSOLVING FLOUR
1	TEASPOON SALT, OR TO TASTE
1	TEASPOON CAYENNE PEPPER, OR TO TASTE, OPTIONAL
1	TABLESPOON PAPRIKA, OPTIONAL

Place one-third of meat in a large saucepan or Dutch oven over medium high heat. Cook until juices evaporate and meat begins to turn brown. Remove from pot and reserve. Repeat until all meat is cooked. Return meat to pot.

Lower heat and add garlic. Cook and stir until garlic softens and the fragrance is compelling. Stir in 6 tablespoons chili powder and cumin, mixing well to coat meat evenly. Add tomato sauce and enough water to just barely cover meat.

Raise heat and bring liquid to a boil. Lower heat and simmer, covered, about 1 hour, or until meat is tender.

While stirring, sprinkle masa harina or flour over chili, 1 tablespoon at a time. Allow chili to cook and thicken between additions. Add masa or flour for desired consistency. Some cooks like soupy chili, others like theirs thick, like stew.

Cook, uncovered, for 20 minutes longer, or until liquid is slightly reduced and thickened. Add salt and cayenne pepper, if desired. Cayenne is quite spicy, so add according to taste.

Stir in paprika for a brighter red color. About 5 minutes before serving, stir in 1 tablespoon chili powder for a fresher chili flavor.

Makes 8 servings.

PINTO BEANS

1	POUND DRY PINTO BEANS
2	CUPS CHOPPED ONION
2	CLOVES GARLIC, CRUSHED
½	CUP HAM OR BARBECUE, CUT IN 1-INCH CHUNKS
4	CUPS WATER
1	FRESH JALAPEÑO, OPTIONAL
1	TEASPOON SALT, OR TO TASTE
3	TABLESPOONS CHOPPED FRESH CILANTRO, OPTIONAL

Rinse beans in a colander. Place in a large saucepan or stockpot with enough water to cover. Soak overnight or place over high heat and bring to a boil. Cook for 1 minute. Turn off heat, cover, and let beans soak for 1 hour.

When beans have finished soaking (either overnight or 1 hour in hot water), pour off soaking liquid. Rinse pot and return beans to pot. Add onions, garlic, meat, and water to cover by 1 inch. Add the jalapeño, if you want the heat.

Bring liquid to a boil over high heat. Lower temperature, cover, and simmer for 2 to 3 hours, or until beans are tender. When beans are tender, add salt to taste.

Just before serving, add cilantro, if desired.

Makes 10 servings.

Variation

For Refried Beans, mash enough beans and small amount of their liquid to make 2 cups; reserve. (May use one 17-ounce can refried beans.) In a skillet over medium heat, cook ½ cup finely chopped onion in 1 tablespoon oil or bacon drippings until light brown, about 7 minutes. Add beans, stirring to mix well. Lower heat. Add some liquid from the beans if a softer consistency is desired. Add ½ teaspoon salt and ⅛ teaspoon pepper, or to taste.

THESE beans are too good to mix with chili. Eat 'em straight, ladled over cornbread. That's the way my brother Buzz Griffith enjoys these beans after he cooks them for about six hours. They're also a wonderful side to barbecue or in a bowl over rice.

BUZZ'S POT *of* BEANS

1	POUND PINTOS
½	POUND BLACK BEANS
½	POUND RED BEANS
3	ONIONS, CHOPPED, TO MAKE ABOUT 6 CUPS (DIVIDED USE)
3	STRIPS BACON, CUT INTO 1-INCH PIECES
2	CUBES CHICKEN BOUILLON
2	TEASPOONS PEPPER
3	TABLESPOONS CHILI POWDER
1	TEASPOON CAYENNE PEPPER
1	WHOLE HEAD OF GARLIC

Rinse beans and pick out any that are shriveled. Pour in a large bowl and add water to cover, at least 3 inches. Soak overnight. Pour off soaking liquid.

Place drained beans in a large stockpot or Dutch oven. Add enough water to cover by 2 inches. Stir in 4 cups chopped onion, bacon, chicken bouillon cubes, pepper, chili powder, and cayenne.

Cut off the end of the garlic pod and pull off white paper-like layers. Leave unpeeled cloves attached to root end. Add to bean pot. Bring liquid to a boil over high heat. Lower heat and simmer, covered, for 2 to 3 hours, until beans are tender.

Add remaining 2 cups onion and cook 2 to 3 hours longer, covered. Add more liquid if necessary. Cook until beans are quite soft. Adjust seasoning to taste.

Makes 12 servings.

- EPAZOTE IS AN HERB THAT HELPS ELIMINATE SOME OF THE GASINESS OF BEANS. IT GROWS WILD IN MUCH OF TEXAS AND MEXICO AND IS BECOMING MORE AVAILABLE IN SUPERMARKETS. IT IS EASIEST TO FIND IN HISPANIC GROCERIES. ADD 1 TABLESPOON CHOPPED FRESH EPAZOTE, OR 1 TEASPOON DRIED, PER POUND OF BEANS.

- FOR A THICKER BROTH, USE THE BACK OF A SPOON TO CRUSH SOME OF THE COOKED BEANS AGAINST THE SIDE OF THE POT. STIR THE MASHED BEANS INTO THE BROTH. REPEAT UNTIL DESIRED THICKNESS IS ACHIEVED.

THIS is another hearty, flavorful soup to add to your list of bowl favorites. There are many versions of this soup. This one has a light stock as a base.

TORTILLA SOUP

½	CUP VEGETABLE OIL (DIVIDED USE)
1	CUP CHOPPED ONION
2	CLOVES GARLIC, CRUSHED
1	(8-OUNCE) CAN TOMATOES WITH GREEN CHILIES
4	CUPS CHICKEN STOCK
1	(8-OUNCE) CAN TOMATO SAUCE
2	TEASPOONS CHILI POWDER
1	TEASPOON GROUND CUMIN
1	TEASPOON SALT, OR TO TASTE
1	TEASPOON PEPPER, OR TO TASTE
4	CORN TORTILLAS, CUT INTO ½ X 1 ½-INCH STRIPS
1 ½	CUPS COOKED CHICKEN, CUT IN BITE-SIZE PIECES
1	CUP MONTEREY JACK CHEESE, GRATED
1	AVOCADO, THINLY SLICED
½	CUP SOUR CREAM
8	LIME WEDGES

Heat 1 tablespoon vegetable oil in a large saucepan or Dutch oven over medium heat. Add onions and garlic; cook until soft. Add tomatoes with green chilies, stock, and tomato sauce.

Stir in chili powder, cumin, salt, and pepper to taste. Reduce heat to low and simmer about 30 minutes.

Meanwhile, heat remaining oil in a small skillet over medium-high heat. Fry tortilla strips in batches until crisp. Drain on paper towels.

Add chicken and bring liquid to a boil. Remove from heat. Ladle soup into bowls and garnish each bowl with tortilla strips, a sprinkling of cheese, a few avocado slices, and a dollop of sour cream. Serve with a lime wedge.

Makes 8 servings.

Fried corn bread, called Hush Puppies, is a classic to serve with fried fish or other seafood. You can't make too many to go with a big pot of Gumbo, either. But they're good with just about any soup, including Chili.

Hush Puppies

2	CUPS YELLOW CORNMEAL
¼	CUP FLOUR
1	TEASPOON BAKING SODA
1	TABLESPOON BAKING POWDER
2	TEASPOONS SALT
1	EGG, LIGHTLY BEATEN
⅓	CUP FINELY CHOPPED GREEN ONION, INCLUDING SOME GREEN PART
1½	CUPS BUTTERMILK
	VEGETABLE OR CORN OIL FOR FRYING

In a large bowl, stir together cornmeal, flour, baking soda, baking powder, and salt. Stir in egg, buttermilk, and onion, mixing just until ingredients are moistened.

Heat 2 inches of oil in a heavy skillet or wide saucepan to 375°. Drop batter by teaspoonfuls into hot oil and fry until golden brown on all sides, turning as necessary. Drain on paper towels.

Makes about 2 dozen.

My dad, Ed Griffith, called it Deer Hunter's Corn Bread or Hot Water Corn Bread, but it is basically fried cornmeal mush. It is most basic of cornmeal concoctions—cornmeal, water, and salt. If they were made "up North," they'd be called Johnnycakes. They're also good with soups, gumbos, and chili. But I remember eating these as a kid on New Year's with a big bowl of Black-Eyed Peas (p. 140). Don't forget the sliced, fresh onion and jalapeños.

HOT WATER CORN BREAD

2	CUPS YELLOW CORNMEAL
1	TEASPOON SALT, OR TO TASTE
1	CUP BOILING WATER
	OIL FOR FRYING
¼	CUP BUTTER, AT ROOM TEMPERATURE, OPTIONAL

Combine cornmeal and salt in a large mixing bowl. Stir in hot water. Dough should be moist enough to hold a shape. Allow dough to cool enough to shape with your hands.

Spoon 1 heaping tablespoon of dough into the palm of one hand. Using both hands, shape the dough into a ½-inch thick oval and place on wax paper.

Heat ½-inch oil in a skillet over medium-high heat. Slide cornbread patties into hot oil and cook until golden and crisp, 3 to 5 minutes. Turn and cook until golden, about 3 minutes longer. Drain on paper towels.

Keep warm. Brush with soft butter, if desired.

Makes 2 dozen.

THIS delicious salad is similar to a taco salad. Hearty and piquant, the queso dressing wilts the lettuce. It can be a meal in itself, with or without the addition of ground beef, shredded barbecue, or shredded chicken.

QUESO SALAD

1	(12-OUNCE) PACKAGE SALAD BLEND (ICEBERG LETTUCE PREFERRED)
½	CUP CHOPPED GREEN ONION, INCLUDING GREEN PART
1	AVOCADO, PEELED, PITTED AND CUT INTO 1-INCH PIECES
1	CUP TOMATO, CUT INTO 1-INCH PIECES
½	CUP CHILE CON QUESO (SEE RECIPE P. 124) OR USE BOTTLED QUESO
2	TABLESPOONS CHICKEN STOCK, OR AS NEEDED
1	CUP COARSELY CRUSHED TORTILLA CHIPS

Toss together iceberg lettuce salad blend, green onion, avocado, and tomato.

Heat Chile con Queso. If needed, add chicken stock to thin to the consistency of a creamy salad dressing. Just before serving, pour warm cheese sauce over salad and toss to coat lettuce. Sprinkle with tortilla chips. Serve immediately.

Makes 6 servings.

Variations

- Crumble ½ pound ground beef into a large skillet over medium heat. Add ¼ teaspoon salt, ½ teaspoon ground cumin, and 1 garlic clove, crushed. Stir and cook until ground beef is well-browned. Drain on absorbent paper towels to remove grease. Add to lettuce along with onion, avocado, and tomato.

- Instead of ground beef, add 1 cup shredded barbecue brisket or shredded chicken (grilled, roasted, or barbecued).

IT only takes one spoonful of Black-Eyed Peas anytime after midnight the first day of the new year for prosperity and general good luck. A bite of peas can't hurt, so don't take any chances. Eat Black-Eyed Peas on New Year's Eve and the first day of the new year.

Black-Eyed Peas are usually served as a side dish. But a bowl full of Black-Eyed Peas makes a great meal, plain, along with a wedge of Corn Bread (p. 138), or over rice. Of course, Texas Caviar (p. 150) also counts for luck on New Year's.

BLACK-EYED PEAS

1	(16-OUNCE) PACKAGE FROZEN BLACK-EYED PEAS WITH SNAPS OR PURPLE HULL PEAS
1	CUP CHOPPED ONION
1	CUP WATER OR CHICKEN STOCK
2	STRIPS BACON, CUT INTO 1-INCH PIECES, OPTIONAL
1	DRIED RED JAPONE CHILE OR 1 FRESH JALAPEÑO, OPTIONAL
1	TEASPOON SALT, OR TO TASTE
1	TEASPOON PEPPER, OR TO TASTE

Combine black-eyed peas, onion, water or stock, bacon, and dried or fresh chile, if desired, in a medium saucepan over medium heat. Bring liquid to a boil, reduce heat to simmer. Cover saucepan and cook until peas are tender, about 30 to 45 minutes, depending on preferred texture.

Make sure too much liquid does not cook away. Black-eyed peas should be almost, but not quite, covered with liquid. When peas are tender, add salt and pepper, to taste.

Makes 8 servings.

Variations

· Soak 2 cups dried black-eyed peas in enough water to cover overnight. Drain soaking water and proceed as above using 4 cups water. Do not add salt until peas are tender. Increase cooking time to 1½ hours, or until tender. Check to make sure liquid does not evaporate during cooking. Add salt to taste.

- For a Cajun touch, add 1½ tablespoons Old Bay (seafood) seasoning and 2 teaspoons red pepper sauce during cooking. Just before serving, add 1½ cups cooked white rice seasoned with 1 teaspoon salt and 1 teaspoon pepper.
- For a Tex-Mex touch, add 1 (10-ounce) can diced tomatoes with green chilies, 2 tablespoons fresh lime juice, and about 6 tablespoons chopped fresh cilantro leaves just before serving.

> I HAVE PEOPLE OVER FOR NEW YEAR'S DAY JUST ABOUT EVERY YEAR. THE MENU VARIES FROM YEAR TO YEAR, BUT THE PEAS ARE ALWAYS THERE. IT IS SURPRISING HOW MANY PEOPLE ARE STILL READY TO PARTY "THE DAY AFTER." PEOPLE COME AND GO WITH NO SET TIME FOR ARRIVAL OR LEAVING. IT'S A GOOD WAY TO CELEBRATE BECAUSE, AT LAST, "THE HOLIDAYS ARE OVER."
>
> *Prissy Shaffer*

NEW YEAR'S DAY is rightfully noted as a day of recovery as well as optimism. Menudo, Mexican tripe stew, is a legendary cure for a hangover. This pungent pot of pig's innards and piquant seasonings will either cure a hangover or, at least, make you forget why your head was spinning and your stomach churning.

MENUDO

2	POUNDS TRIPE
1	PIG'S FOOT, OR 1 POUND PORK NECKBONE
1	BEEF SOUP BONE
1	QUART WATER
1	BAY LEAF
2	CUPS CHOPPED ONION
3	CLOVES GARLIC, CRUSHED
1	TEASPOON BLACK PEPPERCORNS
½	CUP CHILI POWDER
1	TEASPOON CUMIN
2	(15½-OUNCE) CANS HOMINY, WHITE OR YELLOW
1	(10-OUNCE) CAN TOMATOES WITH GREEN CHILIES
1	TEASPOON LEAF OREGANO
1	TEASPOON CAYENNE PEPPER, OR TO TASTE
1	TEASPOON SALT, OR TO TASTE
	GARNISH: LIME WEDGES, CILANTRO LEAVES, CHOPPED GREEN ONION

Cut tripe into 1-inch squares. In large stewpot or Dutch oven, combine tripe, pig's foot or neckbone, water, bay leaf, onion, garlic, and black peppercorns. Bring liquid to a boil, lower heat and simmer, covered, about 2 hours or until tripe is tender.

Remove pig's foot or neckbone. Allow to cool enough to handle and strip off meat; coarsely chop and return meat to pot. Discard bones.

Meanwhile, add chili powder, cumin, hominy, tomatoes with green chilies, oregano, cayenne pepper, and salt to taste. Cook, uncovered, over very low heat another 30 minutes.

Serve in soup bowls with garnish of cilantro and chopped green onions. Pass lime wedges to squeeze into soup.

Makes 8 servings.

Other Ideas
For
New Year's Day

Homestyle Squash Casserole, 19

Mashed Potatoes with Sour Cream and Cream Cheese, 20

Candied Yams, 21

Texas Ambrosia, 26

Sausage and Sauerkraut, 29

Tex-Mex Enchiladas, 30

Macaroni and Cheese, 37

Hot Tamales, 32

Sweet Tamales, 114

Potato Latkes, 49

Sweet and Sour Meatballs, 46

Mexican Hot Chocolate, 117

Christmas Eve Lasagna, 68

Fresh Spinach Salad with Texas Grapefruit, 85

Food Gifts

FOR

THANKSGIVING

THROUGH

NEW YEAR'S DAY

PEANUT BRITTLE, P. 157; (FOREGROUND
FROM RIGHT) WHITE CHOCOLATE FUDGE,
P. 111; MARGARITA BALLS, P. 98

HOMEMADE food gifts are enjoying a renaissance. Not that they ever went out of style. But with so many unique and wonderful products on the shelves of specialty stores, supermarkets, and other retail outlets, it often takes something homemade to convey a truly personal sentiment.

Whether the message is "hello," "thanks" or "happy holiday," this assortment will provide at least one perfect medium for your message. Of course, the best Texas food gift not only tastes good but says "Texas" in style and ingredients.

This chapter is devoted exclusively to traditional gift recipes (see list at left.) However, each of the other chapters has recipes that can also serve as gifts. The list on the next page will whet your appetite and imagination. And remember, you really can't be too Texan when it comes to making and packaging Texas food gifts. There's never a better time to flaunt your Texas pride.

SUGARED PECANS (LEFT) AND
SPICY PECANS, P. 147

THE TEXAS HOLIDAY COOKBOOK

PECANS have a way of showing up in all sorts of recipes, from the beginning to the end of the meal. They're quite simply Texans' favorite nuts. They grow wonderfully well, particularly in the heart of the state. In exchange, Texans have taken them to heart.

Here are sweet and savory versions.

SUGARED PECANS

1	CUP SUGAR
½	TEASPOON CINNAMON
⅛	TEASPOON CREAM OF TARTAR
¼	CUP BOILING WATER
½	TEASPOON VANILLA
1½	CUPS PECAN HALVES

Combine sugar, cinnamon, cream of tartar, and boiling water in a small saucepan over medium heat. Stirring constantly, cook until boiling and boil until candy thermometer reaches 240° (soft-ball stage).

Remove from heat and stir in pecans. Allow to cool a few minutes. Add vanilla and stir until pecans are coated. Pour pecans onto waxed paper and separate.

Makes 2 cups.

SPICY PECANS

1	POUND PECAN HALVES
4	TABLESPOONS BUTTER
1–2	TABLESPOONS WORCESTERSHIRE SAUCE, OR TO TASTE
1	TEASPOON LEMON JUICE
¼	TEASPOON CAYENNE PEPPER OR TO TASTE
2	TEASPOONS SALT, OR TO TASTE

Preheat oven to 200°. Place pecans on a jelly roll pan. Melt butter in a small saucepan over low heat. Remove from heat and add Worcestershire sauce, lemon juice, and cayenne pepper. Mix well and pour over pecans, stirring to coat all sides, and arrange in single layer in pan.

Place in oven and bake for 45 to 60 minutes or until pecans become toasty and brown. Stir occasionally while cooking. Remove from oven and sprinkle with salt to taste, stirring to coat all sides.

Cool completely and store in airtight container for giving. For storage longer than a couple of weeks, place in freezer containers and freeze.

Makes about 4 cups.

Variation

For Salted Pecans, omit cayenne pepper.

WHEN GIVING FOOD GIFTS, INCLUDE STORAGE AND PREPARATION INSTRUCTIONS. FOODS THAT REQUIRE REFRIGERATION SHOULD SAY SO ON THE LABEL. ALSO, REMEMBER TO DATE THE CONTAINER, AS WELL. A COPY OF THE RECIPE IS OFTEN APPRECIATED, TOO.

CUSTOM-BLEND CHILI POWDER AND "YOUR NAME'S" FAVORITE CHILI, P. 149

NOTHING says Texas quite like homemade chili powder. A jar, tin, or packet of your personal blend is a great way to send a taste of the Lone Star State to someone far from home. To truly customize this chili blend, experiment with some of your favorite spices in whatever proportions you prefer.

Custom-Blend Chili Powder

4	OUNCES (ABOUT ½ CUP) GROUND RED CHILIES
1	TABLESPOON GROUND CUMIN
1	TABLESPOON GRANULATED GARLIC
1–2	TEASPOONS CAYENNE PEPPER, OR TO TASTE
2	TEASPOONS POWDERED OREGANO
2	TABLESPOONS PAPRIKA

Combine red chilies, cumin, garlic, cayenne pepper, oregano and paprika. Shake to blend well. Three tablespoons will season 2 pounds of ground beef or coarsely ground beef or venison.

Makes about 1 cup.

"Your Name's" Favorite Chili

2	POUNDS GROUND BEEF OR COARSELY GROUND BEEF OR VENISON FOR CHILI
3	TABLESPOONS CHILI BLEND
1	(8-OUNCE) CAN TOMATO SAUCE
2	CUPS WATER, OR AS NEEDED
2	TABLESPOONS MASA HARINA OR INSTANT DISSOLVING FLOUR

FOR A NICE TOUCH, INCLUDE A COPY OF THE RECIPE WITH THE CUSTOM-BLEND CHILI.

Place ground meat in Dutch oven or large saucepan over medium heat. Cook until meat is no longer pink and liquid has evaporated. Do not brown too much.

Mix in chili blend and stir to coat meat evenly. Add tomato sauce and just enough water to cover meat. Bring liquid to a boil, reduce heat, and simmer, covered, until meat is tender about 1 to 1½ hours.

Dissolve masa or flour in 2 tablespoons water to make a smooth paste. Stir into chili until broth thickens and no lumps remain. Allow to simmer until desired consistency is reached. Adjust seasoning to taste.

Makes 4 to 6 servings.

THIS relish is wonderful as a condiment or dip. It also counts as good luck on New Year's Day.

LONE STAR CAVIAR
(BLACK-EYED PEA RELISH)

SERVING SUGGESTIONS FOR
LONE STAR CAVIAR:

- AS RELISH WITH
  BARBECUE, ROASTED OR
  GRILLED MEATS

- AS A GARNISH FOR
  TOMATO SLICES OR
  GREEN BEANS

- AS A DIP FOR CHIPS OR
  VEGETABLE CRUDITES

1	(16-OUNCE) PACKAGE FROZEN BLACK-EYED PEAS
1	CUP GREEN PEPPER, CHOPPED INTO PIECES ABOUT THE SIZE OF BLACK-EYED PEAS
1	CUP RED BELL PEPPER, CHOPPED INTO PIECES ABOUT THE SIZE OF BLACK-EYED PEAS
¼	CUP FINELY CHOPPED JALAPEÑO PEPPER, RIBS AND SEEDS REMOVED
1	CUP YELLOW ONION, CHOPPED INTO PIECES ABOUT THE SIZE OF BLACK-EYED PEAS
1	CUP FINELY CHOPPED GREEN ONION, INCLUDING GREEN TOPS
2	CLOVES GARLIC, FINELY CHOPPED
1	CUP FINELY CHOPPED PARSLEY
2	TEASPOONS SALT, OR TO TASTE
1	TEASPOON MAPLE SYRUP, OPTIONAL
¾	CUP VEGETABLE OR OLIVE OIL
¼	CUP RED WINE VINEGAR

LONE STAR CAVIAR, SEE
RECIPE ABOVE

THE TEXAS HOLIDAY COOKBOOK

Cook black-eyed peas, according to package instructions, or just until tender, 20 to 30 minutes. Drain well.

Place black-eyed peas in a large mixing bowl. Toss with peppers, onions, garlic, and parsley. Whisk together oil, vinegar, maple syrup and salt. Adjust seasoning to taste. Pour over vegetables and refrigerate overnight to meld flavors.

Place in refrigerator containers for giving. Store up to 2 weeks, refrigerated.

Makes 6 cups.

THIS is a Texas curiosity, but it makes an excellent jelly for roast or grilled meats, especially pork or game. The favorite presentation, however, is to spoon the jelly over a log of cream cheese as a spread for crackers.

JALAPEÑO JELLY

1	CUP CHOPPED GREEN BELL PEPPERS, SEEDED, RIBS AND STEMS REMOVED
⅓	CUP CHOPPED FRESH JALAPEÑO PEPPERS, SEEDED, RIBS AND STEMS REMOVED (WEAR RUBBER GLOVES WHEN HANDLING HOT PEPPERS AND AVOID CONTACT WITH EYES, NOSE OR LIPS)
6	CUPS SUGAR
1½	CUPS APPLE CIDER VINEGAR
1	(6-OUNCE) BOTTLE PECTIN
	GREEN FOOD COLOR, OPTIONAL

Combine bell peppers and jalapeños in work bowl of a food processor. Add vinegar and process until peppers are a smooth puree.

Place in saucepan with sugar over medium-high heat. Bring to a rolling boil and boil for 5 minutes. Remove from heat and pour in pectin. Add color, if desired, to achieve bright, green color. Stir for 2 to 3 minutes. Pour into sterilized jelly jars to within ¼-inch of the rim and seal with manufacturer's lids. Store in refrigerator up to 6 months.

Makes 8 (½-pint) jars.

THIS is hot stuff. The green Jalapeño Jelly pales in comparison because of the heat created by the tiny red chilies called *petins* or *tepins,* depending on who you ask. Small and round, these peppers are available dried year-round. If you can't find them substitute *pequins.* Susan Hamilton Smith of San Antonio grows her own and makes the jelly from fresh peppers that turn from green to red at the end of summer when the days are as hot as the chilies. Handle these carefully, especially fresh ones. The juices can burn fingers, eyes, lips, and noses. Wear gloves, and don't get too close to the fumes.

CHILE PETIN JELLY

¼	CUP FRESH RED CHILE PETINS (OR ⅛ CUP DRIED)
¾	CUP YELLOW BELL PEPPER
6½	CUPS SUGAR
1½	CUPS APPLE CIDER VINEGAR
6	OUNCES LIQUID FRUIT PECTIN

If using fresh chilies, handle carefully. Remove stems from fresh or dried. Remove seeds and ribs from bell pepper. Chop coarsely to make ¾ cup.

Place chilies and bell pepper in the work bowl of a food processor. Pulse on and off to chop fine.

Place chopped chilies in a large saucepan with sugar and cider vinegar. Bring to a boil over high heat and boil for 2 minutes. Remove from heat and allow to cool 5 minutes. Add fruit pectin. Return to high heat and boil for 1 minute.

Pour into 7 (8-ounce) hot sterile jars. Seal and store in refrigerator, up to 6 months.

Makes 7 (8-ounce) jars.

No holiday season is complete without encountering a batch of cereal mix or Texas Trash as it is often called. Go heavy on the pecans, and you'll have it Texas-style.

TEXAS TRASH

1	(15-OUNCE) PACKAGE ROUND OAT CEREAL
1	(12-OUNCE) PACKAGE CRISPY WAFFLE RICE CEREAL
1	(12-OUNCE) PACKAGE CRISPY WAFFLE CORN CEREAL
1	(9-OUNCE) PACKAGE PRETZEL STICKS
2	CUPS PECAN HALVES
1	CUP CASHEWS
2	CUPS PEANUTS
2	CUPS (4 STICKS) BUTTER
½–¾	CUP WORCESTERSHIRE SAUCE, OR TO TASTE
3	TEASPOONS GARLIC SALT, OR TO TASTE
1–2	TEASPOONS RED PEPPER SAUCE, OPTIONAL

In large bowl, toss together cereals, pretzels, and nuts.

Heat oven to 325°. Place butter in a large roasting pan with sides. Melt butter in oven. When butter melts, remove pan from oven and stir in Worcestershire sauce, garlic salt, and red pepper sauce, if desired.

Stir cereal mixture into melted butter, tossing to coat each piece. Place in oven and bake for 30 to 40 minutes, or until cereal is golden brown and crisp.

Store in airtight container for 30 days.

Makes 3 to 3½ quarts.

Salsas are reportedly more popular than ketchup nationwide. It's nice to see the rest of the country catching up to a taste Texans have developed for generations. Here are a couple of versions. The cooked Salsa is the type found in restaurants for dipping crisp tortilla chips. Be careful, you'll fill up before the meal arrives.

Fresh Salsa is similar to pico de gallo, a fresh tomato relish often served with fajitas, strips of grilled beef or chicken.

Try them both; give them both. They'll both stay fresh in the refrigerator for at least a week. The cooked version will last for about a month.

SALSA

1	(28-OUNCE) CAN ITALIAN TOMATOES, WITH JUICE
1	CUP ONION, FINELY CHOPPED
1	TEASPOON FRESH SERRANO PEPPER, SEEDED AND FINELY CHOPPED
2	TABLESPOONS FRESH JALAPEÑO PEPPER, SEEDED AND FINELY CHOPPED
3	CLOVES GARLIC, FINELY CHOPPED
½	TEASPOON SALT, OR TO TASTE
1	TEASPOON SUGAR, OR TO TASTE

Place tomatoes in food processor and pulse on-and-off to finely chop. Add onion, peppers, garlic, salt, and sugar. Pulse 2 to 3 times to blend and achieve desired consistency. Do not puree mixture, but leave small chunks of tomatoes and peppers visible.

Pour into a medium saucepan and place over medium heat. Bring to a boil, lower heat and simmer for 30 minutes, or until slightly thickened. Cool slightly and pour into ½-pint jars. Refrigerate up to 3 to 4 weeks.

Makes 4 (½-pint) jars.

PICO DE GALLO (FRESH SALSA)

4	LARGE, RIPE TOMATOES
	(ABOUT 2 CUPS COARSELY CHOPPED)
2–3	TABLESPOONS FINELY CHOPPED
	FRESH JALAPEÑO PEPPERS, OR TO TASTE
½	CUP ONION, COARSELY CHOPPED
2	CLOVES GARLIC, FINELY CHOPPED
1	TEASPOON SALT, OR TO TASTE
3	TABLESPOONS FRESH CILANTRO,
	FINELY CHOPPED

Combine tomatoes, peppers, onion, and garlic in a medium bowl. Toss to combine. Add salt, mixing well. Allow to stand about 1 hour. Add cilantro, mixing well. Transfer to container with tight-fitting lid. Store in refrigerator up to 1 week.

Makes 2½ cups.

PICO DE GALLO, SEE RECIPE AT LEFT

HOME gardeners take great pride in their pepper patches. A good crop makes plenty of bright green peppers to pickle and stuff into jars for holiday giving.

PICKLED JALAPEÑO PEPPERS

3	POUNDS FRESH JALAPEÑO PEPPERS
½	CUP THINLY SLICED CARROTS
1	CUP ONION, CUT IN WEDGES
6–8	GARLIC CLOVES
2	TABLESPOONS WHOLE BLACK PEPPERCORNS
1	CUP OLIVE OIL
2	CUPS VINEGAR
1	BAY LEAF
¼	TABLESPOON GROUND CUMIN

Leave jalapeños whole or cut into ½-inch thick slices. Place jalapeños, carrot, onion, and garlic in a large stockpot. Cover with water and bring to a boil. Boil 1 minute, then drain.

Sterilize 6 to 8 half-pint jars. Pack peppers evenly into jars, distributing carrot, onion, and garlic garnish among them. Place an equal amount of black peppercorns and olive oil in each jar.

Combine vinegar, bay leaf, and cumin in a small saucepan. Bring to a boil and pour over peppers. Working quickly, seal jars with manufacturer's lids. Cool, then refrigerate. Store in refrigerator for 2 to 3 months.

Makes 6 to 8 (half-pint) jars.

AFTER DINNER, FOR SEVERAL NIGHTS BEFORE CHRISTMAS, MAMA WOULD CLEAR THE TABLE, MAKE LOTS OF HOT CHOCOLATE, AND PUT OUT ALL THE PACKAGE WRAPPINGS: BEAUTIFUL COLORED RIBBONS, PAPER, AND ALL KINDS OF DECORATIONS, INCLUDING MY FAVORITE—GLITTER IN EVERY COLOR IMAGINABLE. AS A LITTLE GIRL, I FELT SO IMPORTANT GETTING TO HELP WRAP THE PACKAGES. THE EDGES HAD TO BE FOLDED JUST RIGHT AND THE SCOTCH TAPE COULDN'T SHOW. DADDY AND MY BROTHER, BILL, WOULD COACH, NODDING APPROVAL AS THEY WATCHED TELEVISION. EVEN NOW I CAN TASTE SOME OF THE GIFTS WE WERE WRAPPING: PUMPKIN BREAD, DIVINITY, FUDGE, AND PECAN PIE.

Dedie Leahy

PEANUT BRITTLE is a long-standing holiday tradition. Making it in the microwave is the easiest method around.

PEANUT BRITTLE

1	CUP RAW PEANUTS, SHELLS AND SKINS REMOVED
½	CUP WHITE CORN SYRUP
1	CUP SUGAR
⅛	TEASPOON SALT
1	TEASPOON VANILLA
1	TEASPOON BUTTER
1	TEASPOON BAKING SODA

Generously butter a cookie sheet. Set aside.

Combine peanuts, corn syrup, sugar, and salt in a 1½- to 2-quart glass measuring dish, preferably one with a handle, like a big measuring cup. Microwave on High for 8 minutes, stirring with a wooden spoon every 2 minutes.

Add butter and vanilla. Microwave on High 2 minutes longer, without stirring. Add baking soda and stir. Working quickly, pour candy mixture onto buttered cookie sheet, in an even layer, distributing peanuts as evenly as possible. Cool completely.

Break into 2- to 3-inch pieces and store in an airtight container.

Makes 15 to 20 pieces.

THESE traditional Southern goodies are wonderful with Spicy Pecans or with any selection of hors d'oeuvres. They're also memorable with a simple soup.

CHEESE STRAWS

1	CUP UNSALTED BUTTER,
	AT ROOM TEMPERATURE
2	CUPS FLOUR
1	TEASPOON SALT
⅛	TEASPOON CAYENNE PEPPER
1	CUP GRATED SHARP CHEDDAR CHEESE

Preheat oven to 350°.

In a medium bowl, combine butter, flour, salt, and cayenne, mixing by hand until smooth. Stir in cheese. Refrigerate 30 minutes to 1 hour for easier handling.

Using about ⅓ of dough, roll thin, about ¼-inch thick. Cut into thin strips, about ½-inch wide and 2-inches long, or load dough into a cookie press and extrude thin strips, about 2-inches long. Place strips on cookie sheet.

Bake for 10 to 15 minutes, or just until golden.

Allow cookie sheet to cool between batches. Repeat until all dough is used.

Makes about 5 dozen.

Variation

Substitute Monterey Jack with jalapeño peppers for grated Cheddar. Omit cayenne pepper.

YET another traditional food gift in Texas is a loaf of pumpkin bread, or any other quick bread.

PUMPKIN BREAD

3⅓	CUPS FLOUR
2	TEASPOONS BAKING SODA
1	TEASPOON NUTMEG
3	TEASPOONS CINNAMON
1	TEASPOON SALT
3	CUPS SUGAR
1	CUP VEGETABLE OIL
⅔	CUP WATER
4	EGGS, WELL-BEATEN
1	(16-OUNCE) CAN PUMPKIN
1	TEASPOON VANILLA
1	CUP COARSELY CHOPPED PECANS
1	CUP RAISINS

Preheat oven to 350°. Grease 3 (8- or 9-inch) loaf pans. For individual gifts, grease 6 to 8 mini-loaf pans.

Sift together flour, baking soda, nutmeg, cinnamon, and salt. In a large bowl, combine sugar, oil, and water. Stir in dry ingredients.

Add eggs, pumpkin, and vanilla, mixing to combine. Do not overbeat. Fold in nuts and raisins. Pour batter into prepared pans. Bake for 55 to 60 minutes, or until toothpick inserted in center comes out clean. Bake mini-loaf pans about 40 minutes, or until loaf tests done.

Makes 3 (8- or 9-inch) loaf pans or 6 to 8 mini-loaf pans.

INDEX